AMSTRAD GR
– the advanced user guide

Robert Ransom

SIGMA PRESS

ISBN 1-85058-040-5

Published by:
SIGMA PRESS
98A Water Lane
Wilmslow
Cheshire
U.K.
Printed in Malta by Interprint Limited

Distributors:

U.K., Europe, Africa:
JOHN WILEY & SONS LIMITED
Baffins Lane, Chichester
West Sussex, England

Australia:
JOHN WILEY & SONS INC.
GPO Box 859, Brisbane
Queensland 40001
Australia

Reprinted 1987

Acknowledgements: CPC−464, CPC−664 and CPC−6128 are the Trade Marks of Amstrad Consumer Electronics plc.

Preface

This book is about graphics for Amstrad home computers, specifically the CPC 464 CPC 664 and CPC 6128 machines. These computers are ideally suited for graphics work for a number of reasons. Firstly, the version of BASIC included in ROM is very fast, enabling the user to perform numeric calculations or to draw lines more quickly than is possible with many other home computers. Next, the graphics screen is mapped as a 640 X 400 unit area. This is a similar resolution to many professional quality graphics devices (although the 'true' Amstrad resolution is actually 640 X 200 pixels, as you will see in Chapter 1). The most important advantage of the Amstrad home computers for graphics use is probably the range of graphics commands available for use from within the BASIC language. Unlike the hapless owner of a Commodore 64 machine, the Amstrad owner can draw lines, change screen and plotting colours, and even paint areas of the screen (CPC 664 only) without recourse to an endless series of PEEKs and POKEs to memory locations.

The present book is intended as a simple introduction to computer graphics for the novice programmer as well as a more detailed primer introducing the world of real computer graphics: the sort that are used in computer-aided design, simulation work and art studies. Much of the basic groundwork covered in these pages is relevent to sophisticated graphics software packages running on computers costing hundreds of thousands of pounds.

In the following pages you will learn how to construct simple pictures and graphs using text screen characters, to draw and manipulate two and three dimensional 'wireframe' line objects, to draw in perspective, to use 'hidden line' algorithms, to construct multisegment pictures, and to fill in frame diagrams to give a solid high resolution picture. A variety of programs will be given as examples, and a library of subroutines will be built up to allow you to develop your own 'graphics library' using the same techniques. It is assumed that the reader has written at least a few simple programs in BASIC, and has a grasp of Amstrad BASIC commands. The Amstrad manuals are all quite detailed enough for understanding of the general programming techniques used in this book, but if you wish to go further I recommend the *CPC464 Advanced User Guide* by Mark Harrison, also published by Sigma Press.

Although an understanding of computer graphics relies on some understanding of the mathematics involved, you will be able to use the routines without knowing any coordinate geometry or matrix algebra. This is possible because the purpose of each routine is clearly described, together with details of input and output variables. For the more mathematically adept reader, an appendix describing the matrix manipulations involved is included.

I have tried to make the material in this book as accessible as possible for owners of Amstrad home computers. The program examples in these pages have been developed on a CPC 664 with colour monitor, and will run identically on the CPC 6128. There are only a few subtle differences between CPC 664 and 464, so no difficulty will be experienced by the reader armed with the disk-driveless machine. There is even no distinction between disk and tape owner - the input and output commands in Locomotive Softwares' excellent BASIC interpreter are identical for both.

As this book concerns itself almost entirely with Amstrad computer graphics, you may like some advance information on how the book's graphics were themselves prepared. In the main, the figures are from two sources. The program output was obtained using an Epson MX 82F/T printer coupled via a Centronics interface cable to the user port of a CPC-664. The software to drive the interface was obtained from two different sources: the first is a machine code listing by F M Collins to be found in the April 1985 issue of Practical Computing (this program required a few modifications to run with the Epson printer). A more sophisticated package of screen dump software is Tascopy, and this has been extensively used here. You will find details of Tascopy in Chapter 1.

Some of the diagrams were obtained using a rather more heavyweight approach. A Digital Equipment Corporation (DEC) Vax 11/780 'supermini' computer was used for this purpose, and programs to generate the Figures were written in Fortran 77, utilizing Tektronix Plot-10 graphics software. This software consists of a set of Fortran callable subroutines to perform graphics operations. The actual figures were obtained on a Tektronix 4663 flatbed two pen plotter. This choice of equipment (about £250,000 worth) was really only made because of its availability, together with the practical consideration that I had no suitable plotter attached to my Amstrad. A more detailed discussion of the merits and features of printers and plotters can be found in Chapter 1.

The use to which the graphics techniques in this book will be put by the reader depends very much on individual circumstances. Although many people already have an idea what they want from graphics, the author hopes that the techniques set out here will stimulate interest in the possibilities of graphics on Amstrad home computers. This book can be used on several different levels. If you only want to have some programs which show interesting graphics effects to impress your friends, then you will find the book a source of useful program material. I do hope, however, that many readers will want to go further than this, and will be willing to try to understand the basic principles behind computer graphics. You will find that many of the programs included here may be enhanced by additions, extensions or even merging into program 'packages'. I have tried to keep the programs in discrete sections that are as straightforward as possible, so I've avoided this kind of 'integrated software' approach in the interests of clarity.

Let me wish you good luck, and I hope that you will get as much enjoyment out of exploring the graphics capabilities of your computer as I have had in writing this book. If you find mistakes or errors, please let me know, and if you have success in amending the programs, well, perhaps you'll let me know about your triumphs as well. Now, I'm going to try some different parameter values for those fractal curves....

I have received help from several sources during the preparation of the book. Ray Matela first introduced me to the world of computer graphics, and I've learnt a lot from his extensive experience. I'd also like to thank Greg Turk for permission to use an amended version of his Apple fractal program (thanks also to Peter Sorensen), and thanks to Tektronix Inc (Beaverton, Oregon) for permission to copy Figures 7.1 and 7.6 from their Plot 10 3D User's Support Manual. Graham Beech of Sigma Press encouraged me to consider the Amstrad computers for graphics work, (and loaned me a CPC 664 to develop the programs for this book), and finally thanks to my wife and children for allowing me to lock myself away for long hours at a time.

Robert Ransom

Woburn Sands
July 1985

Special Note for
CPC 464
Users

– see following page

INFORMATION FOR
CPC 464 USERS

**THE FOLLOWING COMMANDS WILL NOT FUNCTION ON THE
CPC 464**

GRAPHICS PEN - **remove this command** when using the CPC 464
GRAPHICS PAPER - **remove this command** when using the CPC 464
FRAME - replace with **CALL & BD19**

**THE FOLLOWING COMMANDS HAVE AN 'INK MODE'
PARAMETER NOT AVAILABLE ON THE CPC 464.**

DRAW
DRAWR
PLOT
PLOTR
MOVE
MOVER

When these commands are encountered with 4 parameters, for example

DRAW 50,100,2,N

The line must be rewritten as

PRINT CHR$(23);CHR$(N):DRAW 50,100,2:PRINT CHR$(23);CHR$(0)

THE COMMAND

PEN

**HAS A 'BACKGROUND MODE' PARAMETER NOT AVAILABLE ON
THE CPC 464.** When you encounter PEN with 3 parameters, for example

PEN #1,2,N

The line must be rewritten as

PRINT CHR$(22);CHR$(N):PEN #1,2:PRINT CHR$(22);CHR$(0)

CONTENTS

PROGRAM INDEX

The following annotated list of programs is included in order to help you see at a glance what your computer will be able to do after you have typed in the listings in this book. All the programs have been tested on Amstrad computers and should work satisfactorily. Note that some listings are meant to be **MERGEd** with main programs already loaded into your computer. These amendments are marked with an asterisk here.

Note also that the program listings were done on an EPSON printer which substitutes the character '£' for '#' throughout. You should, therefore, replace each of these characters as you procede.

Chapter 1   **BLOCK**
A program demonstrating use of low resolution block graphics to create a picture.

COLOUR
Shows the colours available on the Amstrad computers as a series of grey shades outputted to a printer.

HEXAGON
A simple program that draws a hexagon. The program demonstrates simple the setting up of the high resolution screen and line drawing commands.

CIRCLE
Another simple program, this time showing how a simple formula can be used to generate a regular shape.

SPIRAL
A spiral generation program.

GRAPH

A demonstration program that can be used to draw graphs. The graph scales, labels and data are inputted during program execution.

SCREEN
A program that outlines the screen dimensions to test the picture size on a printer (if a printer is available!)

Chapter 2   **NOWYOUSEEIT**
This program demonstrates the drawing and erasing of lines to produce the effect of movement.

INVERT
A program demonstrating the effect of inverting pixels rather than drawing and erasing them.

JOIN
Tests pixels to prevent lines crossing.

MASKDEMO
Demonstrates the use of the CPC664 and CPC6128 MASK command.

DASH
A dashed line generating program for CPC464 owners

ELLIPSE
An ellipse generation program.

SINE
A program for generating sine waves.

PARA
A program to generate parabolic curves.

VECTOR
Program showing drawing and erasure of line vectors to produce animation.

FRACTAL
A demonstration of the striking patterns that can be obtained by plotting fractal curves.

Chapter 3   **EASYDRAW**
Program demonstrating the use of data structures for defining 2D data.

FILE2D
This program allows you to create files containing point and line data to draw 2D pictures. The version here stores files on disk, but instructions for tape storage are given in the text.

DRAW2D

An extended version of **EASYDRAW** which inputs data from a disk or tape file (created using **FILE2D**).

SKETCH

Program allowing interactive creation of a 2D data set on screen, using joystick to control cursor movement.

Chapter 4 **ROTATE**

Shows movement of an arrow to demonstrate 2D rotations.

TRV1, TRV2, TRV3

These programs are developed from **ROTATE**, and are built up throughout the chapter to handle general 2D transformations.

V1 rotation + translation (arrow)

V2 rotation + translation + scaling (spaceship)
V3 as V2 but reads in data from a sequential file created using **SKETCH**, and uses a matrix multiplication method.

ZOOM

Demonstrates the use of a clipping algorithm to allow zooming in and out of a picture.

QUADRANT *

A version of **SKETCH** which allows an object 4X screen size to be drawn. This program is especially useful for preparing data files containing maps etc. and is used in conjunction with **ZOOMQUAD** below.

ZOOMQUAD *

A version of **ZOOM** which manipulates the full 1280 X 800 data area made available by **QUADRANT**.

Chapter 5 **PIE**

A program to generate pie charts: can be used in any **MODE**.

EXPLODE

A version of **PIE** allowing individual sectors to be displaced or 'exploded'.

MINIPIE
A version of PIE allowing multiple 'pies' to be displayed at the same time.

SUPERG
An expanded version of the GRAPH program in Chapter 1. Can be used to plot data points or to draw a continuous line.

CHART
A graphing program with months labelled on the X axis.

EMPHASIS ★
A version of CHART allowing comparison of two sets of data.

CUMUL ★
A version of CHART showing cumulative plotting of two sets of data.

BAR ★
A version of CHART plotting bars instead of data points.

PATTERN
A program for shading rectangles with a variety of hatch patterns.

HATCH ★
An addition for BAR to allow hatch patterns to be used in bar charts.

BARCOMP ★
A version of BAR plotting two sets of bar chart data on the same axes.

HISTO3D
A program for generating three dimensional histograms.

Chapter 6   DESIGN
This is a computer aided design program which may be used in a variety of situations where objects have to be fitted into a space: room layout, circuit design, etc.

Chapter 7   FILE3D
This program is an expanded version of FILE2D (Chapter 3),

and allows you to create 3D data files.

SKETCH3D *
An amended version of SKETCH Chapter 3) allowing interactive 'creation' of a 3D data file 'on screen'.

PROJ3D
This program draws a picture using 3D data. The program may either be used in conjunction with a 3D datafile on tape or disk, or can use data statements within the program itself.

TRANS3D
Program consisting of the basic PROJ3D section, with a routine for three dimensional rotation. Routines for scaling and translation are also given in the text.

PER3D
This is an extended version of PROJ3D which draws 3D wire frame pictures in perspective.

BILL *
An amendment of PER3D that allows a two dimensional data set to be projected as a 'billboard' in three dimensions.

Chapter 8   **PAINTER**
A program demonstrating use of the painter's algorithm for removing hidden surfaces from a picture.

FILE3DH
This version of FILE3D incorporates additional input statements to handle the additional surface data elements needed to draw a hidden lines picture.

HIDDEN
The main hidden lines removal program, allowing hidden lines to be removed from a single convex object with the origin inside the object.

S3DH *
A version of SKETCH3D which adds surface information to the 3D data set created.

HIDDEN2 *
This version of HIDDEN can be used with S3DH to create a

hidden lines image of a data set 'expanded' from two dimensions.

Chapter 9   MOL3D
A program for drawing molecules with atoms represented as circles 'spheres') in 3D space.

INPUTMOL
This programs creates the molecule data file read by MOL3D containing X,Y,Z coordinate data for each atom together with the atomic radius.

Appendix 2

MATRIX MULTIPLICATION 1
MATRIX MULTIPLICATION 2

Two routines for multiplying 1 X 3 by 3 X 3, and 3 X 3 by 3 X 3 matrices respectively.

Chapter One

Introduction

1.1 What are computer graphics?

Computer graphics are the visual representation of the numeric information encoded within a computer. Although normal text output on the computer screen is, in the strictest sense, 'graphics', computer graphics really begin when graphs, histograms, pictures and animations are displayed.

In the days before home computers, computer graphics were limited to industrial and educational mainframe computers whose users could budget tens of thousands of dollars on hardware and software. Today, however, the tables have turned and home microcomputers have a great advantage over mainframe computers: on most micros, graphics facilities are built into both hard and software, while mainframe users have to separately purchase terminals and software on which to run graphics programs, and these items don't come cheap! The advantage of large computers lies of course in the speed at which they can do things and the amount of memory available to the programmer. We will return at intervals throughout this book to make comparisons between graphics on mainframe and microcomputers, but let us now turn to look at the nuts and bolts of computer graphics, before homing in on the Amstrad home computers as the vehicles for our graphics studies.

1.2 The elements of computer graphics

The single main element which has aided the flourishing of graphics facilities on home micros is the development of raster display technology. In the early days of computer graphics, graphic primitives (points, lines, filled areas) were drawn by direct control of the beam in the cathode ray tube being used. This kind of display (called vector display) is still used in professional graphics where high accuracy is needed. Although such devices are great fun to use, you won't find many coupled to home micros. This is because they are expensive and have the additional limitation that you often cannot selectively erase lines on this kind of device: you can only wipe the whole screen at one fell swoop.

More recently, refresh displays have come into prominence. Refresh displays get around the shortcomings of vector displays very neatly. First of all, refresh technology is TV technology, so you can buy a new monochrome display device for £40. Also, the very term 'refresh' indicates that the picture is constantly being renewed: on a standard TV it is replaced 30 times each second. This means that you can wipe out a line and redraw it in another place 'quicker than the eye can see'. In actual fact this is easier in theory than practice, because you have got to make the visual information available for the computer to act on. This visual information is held in the form of a parcel of computer memory called a display file. The display file is essentially a 'map' of the displayable points on the screen. Each of these points is called a pixel (short for picture element), and each pixel requires a storage location in the display file.

In the simplest form of display file, only one bit is used to represent each pixel. (Which is why you will often find the display file on micros referred to as a 'bitmap'). If the bit is set to one, the pixel is lit, if it is set to zero, it remains unlit. This representation is ideal for a monochrome display without grey shades), because each point can only be dark or light. If a number of colours or grey shades are to be drawn, more than one bit must be available to represent each pixel. If you ever have occasion to enter the world of professional graphics, you will find the term 'bit plane' used. Each bit plane is an extra bit used per pixel. Two bit planes gives four possible pixel colour combinations, three bit planes gives seven combinations and so on.

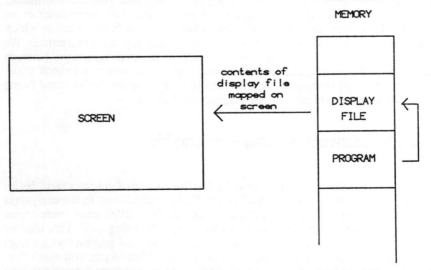

Figure 1.1 Relationship between the screen and computer memory. The program manipulates the screen locations 'bitmapped' in the display file, and the computer hardware refreshes the screen image of the display file 30 times a second.

Let us recap on the terms we have introduced so far. The important ones are refresh display, display file, pixel, and bitmap. You will need to remember these because they crop up a lot in graphics lore.

Now at this point you may be worrying about how the information gets from the display file to the screen, or indeed about how the display file is itself structured. On the first problem the simple answer is: forget it. If you really want to know about addressing rasters and so on then you need a hardware manual and not this book. The structure of the display file however is relevent, but is highly machine specific.

We have not yet finished with our overview of graphics concepts. The next term to introduce is the resolution of the graphic screen. You will be familiar with the terms 'hi-res' and 'lo-res' graphics. In hi-res mode, the resolution is defined by the number of pixels that can be displayed on the screen. A resolution of 1000 X 400 pixels means that 400,000 pixels can be displayed. You can work out the massive display file that would be needed to cope with this resolution even in monochrome: it is 400000/8 bytes (one bit per pixel) or 50K bytes. No wonder home micros work on lower resolutions!

The Amstrad home micros have a maximum hi-res screen resolution of 640 X 200 pixels, which needs a display file of 16K bytes. In fact, as you will see below, all high resolution modes on the CPC 6128,664 and 464 need 16K bytes space: the difference is that some modes give a larger range of colours for the sacrifice of resolution.

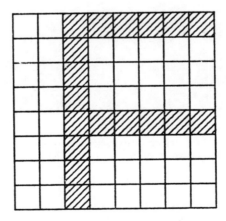

Figure 1.2 The 'low resolution' character grid is made up of a square measuring 8 X 8 pixels. Each standard character is mapped in a special section of memory accessed when a character is to be printed on screen.

17

Low resolution graphics are based around blocks of pixels which are considered as integral units. The Amstrad version of these blocks measures eight bits by eight bits, or 1 X 1 bytes as you can see in the diagram.

The principle use of low resolution graphics is for text, but the block graphics facility uses the same block space and allows the programmer to design quite striking graphic effects using the low resolution screen only. The block graphics characters available on your Amstrad are listed in your User Manual. There are two techniques for using these symbols. First, they can be 'pasted' on the screen to produce the image you want, say a backdrop for a computer game (Figure 1.3). Alternatively, they may be directly used in animation (graphics for 'matchstick men' and 'space invaders' are provided, for example).

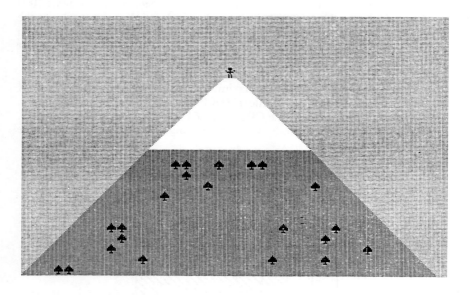

Figure 1.3 An example of a picture made up of character cells or 'block graphics'. This simple picture consists of special characters placed on screen using the LOCATE command.

The picture in Figure 1.3 was produced using just five different block graphics symbols. As you can see from the program below, the 'mountain', 'trees' and 'Chris Bonnington' are all drawn using the PRINT CHR$ command. The LOCATE command is used to place the graphics symbols at the correct row and column on the screen.

BLOCK program

```
10 REM BLOCK GRAPHICS DEMONSTRATION
20 REM TO DRAW A PRETTY SCENE IN MODE 1
30     MODE 1
40     INK 0,11:INK 1,0:INK 2,13:INK 3,9
50     CLS
60 REM FIRST DRAW MOUNTAIN
70     PEN 3:REM DRAW MOUNTAIN IN GREEN
80     J=26
90     FOR I=1 TO 19
100      IF J<15 THEN PEN 2
110      J=J-1
120      LOCATE I,J
130      PRINT CHR$(214)
140        FOR K=1 TO J-I+13
150           LOCATE I+K,J
160           IF J<14 THEN PEN 2
170           IF RND(1)<0.1 THEN GOSUB 300 ELSE PAPER 0:PRINT CHR$(143)
180        NEXT K
190        LOCATE I+K,J
200        PRINT CHR$(215)
210    NEXT I
220 REM NOW DRAW MOUNTAINEER
230      PEN 1
240      FIG=247
250      FIG=FIG+1:IF FIG=252 THEN FIG=248
260      LOCATE 20,6
270      PRINT CHR$(FIG)
280      FOR I=1 TO 500:NEXT I:GOTO 250
290 STOP
300 REM SUBROUTINE TO PLOT TREES
310      IF K=1 OR K=J-I+13 THEN PAPER 0:PRINT CHR$(143):RETURN
320      IF J<14 THEN PEN 2:PRINT CHR$(143):RETURN
330      PEN 1:REM DRAW OBJECTS IN BLACK
340      PAPER 3:REM SET OBJECT BACKGROUND TO GREEN
350      PRINT CHR$(229)
360      PAPER 2
370      PEN 3
380 RETURN
```

This program represents the first and last use of non-text block graphics in this book. If all you really want to do is to program simple games using these symbols, there are plenty of other books that will show you how!

1.3 Amstrad screen modes

Although the maximum Amstrad screen resolution is 640 * 200 pixels, your machine can work in three different resolution modes. These modes (MODE 0, MODE 1, MODE 2) give effective working resolutions of 160 * 200 pixels, 320 * 200 pixels, and 640 * 200 pixels respectively. In addition, the Amstrad screen is actually 'mapped' as a 640 * 400 unit area in all modes. This means that each pair of units along the Y ≐ vertical) axis will actually refer to the same pixel. The units along the X axis are more flexible. Working in MODE 2, each unit is equivalent to one pixel. In MODE 1, each pair of units equals one pixel, while in MODE 0, four units share the same pixel.

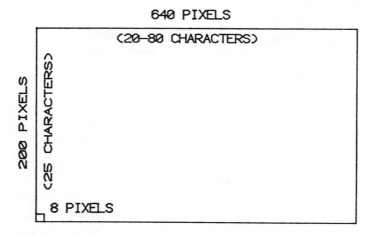

Figure 1.4 The high resolution and low resolution screens compared. Each character is actually drawn as an 8 X 8 sequence of pixels.

I should make two clarifying points about this apparent confusion. First, the use of a 640 * 400 unit work area gives the correct aspect ratio to the X and Y axes, and the fact that the units are the same in all modes vastly simplifies switching between modes. The second point involves the use of the lower resolution modes, 1 and 0. Why use them at all? The answer to this question lies in the use of colour. If the true number of pixels in a 16K display memory is 640 * 200, there will be one bit per pixel, only enough to specify one of two colours (background or foreground). If the pixel number is 320 * 200, two bits of display memory can be dedicated to each pixel, thus allowing four possible colour combinations. With a pixel number of 160 * 200, two further bits are released per pixel, giving 16 colour combinations on screen at the same time.

As you progress through this book you will see (and I hope use) many different programs involving the various screen modes. Before leaving the topic of modes it might however be useful to consider the display of the text character blocks at each mode. If you look in the Appendices of your Amstrad manual you will see the various characters available. These characters are drawn ocupying the 8 * 8 character cell we discussed earlier in this chapter. If you type a character in either MODE 0 or MODE 2, it is clear that the character does not occupy a square block. In MODE 2, each character does appear square. Now the vertical (Y) resolution in all modes is 200 pixels, and each character cell is eight units high. Dividing 200/8 gives 25 lines on screen IN ALL MODES. Now consider the horizontal (X) resolution. In MODE 2, 640/8 = 80 characters can be displayed. In MODE 1, 320/8 = 40 characters can be displayed. In MODE 0, 160/8 = 20 characters can be displayed.

In this book we will concentrate on graphics applications written in BASIC, and you will not therefore have to worry about the implementation of memory mapping in the CPC 6128, CPC 664 and CPC 464. If you do wish to program graphics in machine code, you should purchase the CPC464 Firmware Guide (AMSOFT 158), available from Amstrad.

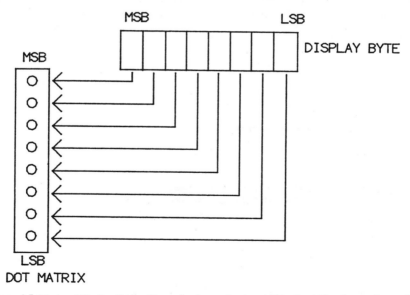

Figure 1.5 A byte within the display file can be dumped onto a printer by setting the needles on the printhead to copy the on/off state of each pixel in the byte. On Epson series printers the dot matrix head is an 8 X 1 needle band, so each byte is directly translated into a vertical column of dots. MSB = most significant bit (ie 128), LSB = least significant bit (ie 1).

The high resolution display file is more versatile than just providing a bitmap for the video screen. It can also be used to provide data for a display device. If a dot-matrix printer is used, a 'screen dump' can be performed to transfer the information in the display file onto paper by sequentially writing each byte like this

A plotter works on a rather different principle, and bypasses the display file altogether: lines are drawn between points directly specified to the plotter. The quality of the graphics produced can be very high as each line is a true line and not a sequence of tiny dots. Four of the first five figures of the book so far were done on a plotter.

1.4 Inks and colours

Probably the most confusing aspect of running programs on Amstrad computers is the choice of colour. As we have already seen, two colours are available in MODE 2, four colours can be displayed in MODE 1, and a spectacular 16 colours in MODE 0. The total 'palette' of colours is 27, and you can see the full range by entering and running the following program

COLOUR program

```
10 REM ****COLOUR CHECK PROGRAM****
15 MODE 0
20 COL1=0:COL2=15
27 PAPER 0
30 CLS
32 IF COL1=0 THEN LOCATE 1,2:PRINT"COLOUR CHART PAGE 1"
33 IF COL1=16 THEN LOCATE 1,2:PRINT"COLOUR CHART PAGE 2"
35 M=-1
40 K=0:L=0
45 LOCATE 1,5
50 FOR J=COL1 TO COL2
55 M=M+1
60 INK M,J
70 NEXT J
130 FOR I=0 TO (COL2-COL1)*40
140 IF L>40 THEN L=1:K=K+1
150 L=L+1
160 GRAPHICS PEN K
170 MOVE I,0
```

```
180 DRAW I,300
190 NEXT I
200 IF COL2=27 THEN 200
205 IF COL1=0 THEN PRINT"PRESS KEY FOR MORE"
210 COL1=16:COL2=27:M=-1
215 INK 15,0
216 PAPER 15
217 A$=INKEY$
218 IF A$=""THEN 217
220 GOTO 30
```

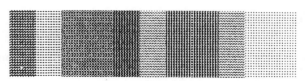

Figure 1.6 Output from the COLOUR program. The screen dump was performed using Tascopy software, showing grey shades for the different colours. Note that MODE 0 is used to give up to 16 colours on screen at the same time. The numbers were added after printing (MODE Ø numbers are too large).

23

You will see that some of the colours in fact look very similar. This is due mainly to the shortcomings of your monitor rather than to a bad choice of colour on the part of Amstrad plc. Of course you may be using a monochrome monitor restricting colour to a range of 'grey shades'. If you do not have a colour monitor, fear not! Most if not all the programs in this book will still be of value to you.

Amstrad colours are coded by the INK command. This command is used as follows

```
INK 0,1
```

where the first number is the ink code number and the second number is the colour number as specified in your CPC 464 User Manual or on the disk drive housing of your CPC 664/CPC 6128. Merely specifying an INK colour like this will only have an immediate effect if you specify an ink code of 0 or 1. Ink code 0 sets the screen colour (by default), while ink code 1 sets the default drawing colour, so all lines and characters will be set to this colour unless otherwise specified.

You can change the INK code for drawing, background colour or screen border colour by using the commands

```
PEN n
PAPER n
BORDER n
```

where n is the chosen ink code. The PAPER command requires a little more explanation. It only affects the environment of text characters. If you wish to change the screen colour you need to use the command

```
INK 0,n
```

where n is the required screen colour.

1.5 Some simple graphics

Now that you can manipulate the screen colours, we are ready to look at some simple graphics programs.

We will start our graphics excursions with four simple programs to give the flavour of high resolution graphics. The first three of these programs, which draw a hexagon, a circle and a spiral, all use the basic graphics primitives - points and lines - which will be discussed at length in Chapter 2. The last example, GRAPH, uses graphics mixed with text.

First we will draw a hexagon. The data for the hexagon is given in the form of X,Y pairs of coordinates, as you will see from the data statements. Do not worry too much if terms like 'coordinate' seem unfamiliar: the programs below are really very simple and we will spend more time on terminology later.

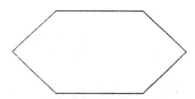

Figure 1.7 Output from HEXAGON

HEXAGON program

```
10 REM ****PROGRAM HEXAGON****
20 REM TO CONSTRUCT A HEXAGON USING DATA STATEMENTS FOR COORDINATE DATA
30 INK 0,0
40 INK 1,12
50 MODE 1
60 PAPER 0
70 GRAPHICS PEN 1:REM LINES 30-70 SET UP DRAWING COLOURS
80 READ X1,Y1
90 FOR I=1 TO 6
100 X=X1:Y=Y1
110 READ X1,Y1
120 MOVE X,Y
130 DRAW X1,Y1
140 NEXT I
150 END
160 DATA 100,150,200,150,250,100,200,50,100,50,50,100,100,150
```

As this is the first real 'graphics' program in the book we will step through it line by line, even though it really is very simple. Lines 10 and 20 are common-or-garden rem statements. Lines 30 and 40 set background (screen) and foreground (pen) colours. Line 50 sets **MODE 1**, and line 60 confirms that the text paper colour will be the same as the screen colour. In line 0 we read in the 'start' coordinates for the hexagon, in this case the top left hand corner has been chosen, but any of the corners could have been selected. The start coordinates are placed in variables X1, Y1. This is a temporary measure! We really need the coordinates to be in variables X,Y as you will see in line 120. Line 90 is the start of the loop for drawing the lines. This loop is executed six times, once for each line. Line 100 puts the values of X1,Y1 into X,Y. This is because the end of the previous line becomes the start of the next line.

The coordinates of the point at the end of the line to be drawn next are then read in (line 110), and lines 120-130 are the instructions for drawing the line itself. The line is drawn from X,Y to X1,Y1. Line 140 marks the end of the loop, and line 160 contains the coordinate data to draw the hexagon.

The HEXAGON program illustrates the use of several simple graphics techniques: the use of the **MOVE** and **DRAW** commands, setting up the screen colours, and rudimentary graphics data handling. In HEXAGON, all the data is absolutely defined by the programmer. The next short program, CIRCLE, uses a different technique: here, the data is generated by a mathematical function, in this case the position of points on a fixed radius from a centre point.

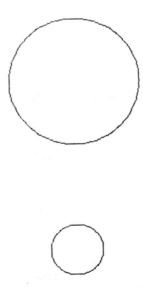

Figure 1.8 Output from CIRCLE

Although the program draws an approximate circle, it really draws a 100-gon by computing the positions of 100 points sequentially around the centre. CIRCLE is crude, slow, and only for demonstration purposes: it is perhaps a curious fact that Amstrad BASIC does not actually support a CIRCLE command, common with many other varieties of BASIC running on other machines. This is a rather insignificant shortcoming on what is otherwise an excellent machine (and anyhow it gives us the excuse to play with circle drawing algorithms!)

CIRCLE program

```
10 REM ****PROGRAM CIRCLE****
20 REM TO CONSTRUCT CIRCLE FROM CALCULATED COORDINATES
30 INK 0,0
40 INK 1,12
50 MODE 1
60 PAPER 0
70 GRAPHICS PEN 1:REM LINES 30-70 SET UP DRAWING COLOURS
80 INPUT"RADIUS?";R
90 AN=0
100 AI=0.062831853
110 X1=R*COS(AN):Y1=R*SIN(AN)
120 FOR I=1 TO 100
130 X=X1:Y=Y1
140 AN=AN+AI
150 X1=R*COS(AN):Y1=R*SIN(AN)
160 MOVE X+320,Y+200
170 DRAW X1+320,Y1+200
180 NEXT I
190 END
```

The next program also uses a mathematical function to generate a shape, in this case a spiral. SPIRAL doesn't do much more than CIRCLE, but it can give some aesthetic-looking patterns if you set R E (the 'resolution') large enough.

```
10 REM ****PROGRAM SPIRAL****
20 REM TO CONSTRUCT A SPIRAL FROM CALCULATED COORDINATES
30 INK 0,0
40 INK 1,12
50 MODE 1
60 PAPER 0
```

```
70 GRAPHICS PEN 1:REM LINES 30-70 SET UP DRAWING COLOURS
80 INPUT"RESOLUTION?";RE
90 X1=320:Y1=200
100 FOR I=0 TO 50 STEP RE
110 R=I*2:X=X1:Y=Y1
120 X1=R*SIN(I)+320:Y1=R*COS(I)+200
130 MOVE X,Y
140 DRAW X1,Y1
150 NEXT I
```

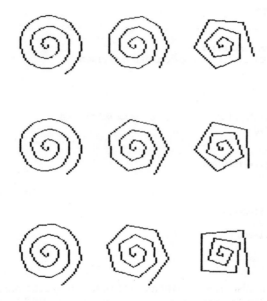

Figure 1.9 Output from SPIRAL. Nine different values of RE have been used

The next program uses the basic graphics primitives to create a graph. The graph scales, axis legends and coordinate points are inputted during program execution. The program could easily be amended to read data from a tape or disk file, or to display more than one set of data. (The access of sequential data storage files is discussed in Chapter 3).

28

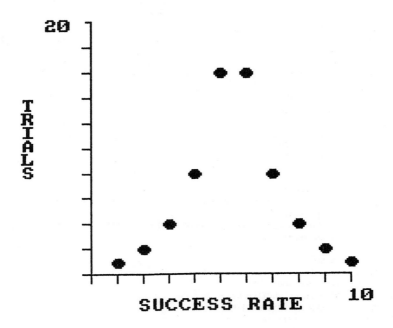

Figure 1.10 Output from GRAPH

GRAPH program

```
10 REM ****PROGRAM GRAPH****
20 REM TO DRAW A SIMPLE LABELLED GRAPH
30    INK 0,13
40    INK 1,0
50    MODE 1
60    INPUT"HOW MANY POINTS ON THE GRAPH?";P
70 DIM X(P),Y(P)
80    FOR I=1 TO P
90    INPUT"XVAL?";X(I)
100   INPUT"YVAL?";Y(I)
110   NEXT I
120   INPUT"WHAT IS MAX VALUE ON X AXIS?";MX
130   INPUT"WHAT IS MAX VALUE ON Y AXIS?";MY
140   INPUT"X AXIS NAME";N$
150   INPUT"Y AXIS NAME";M$
155 CLS
```

29

```
160 REM NOW DRAW THE AXES
170      MOVE 200,380
180      DRAW 200,80
190      DRAW 500,80
200 REM PUT IN SCALE MARKS
210   FOR I=1 TO 11
220      MOVE 190,(I*30)+50
230      DRAW 200,(I*30)+50
240   NEXT I
250   FOR I=1 TO 11
260      MOVE (I*30)+170,70
270      DRAW (I*30)+170,80
280   NEXT I
290 REM NOW LABEL AXES
300 REM POSITION X LABEL FIRST
305 REM START POSITION IS CENTRE PT ON X AXIS MINUS HALF STRING LENGTH
310   AX=(350-((LEN(N$)*16)/2))
315 REM START POSITION IS CENTRE PT ON Y AXIS PLUS HALF STRING LENGTH
320   AY=(240+((LEN(M$)*16)/2))
330 TAG
340      MOVE AX,50
350   PRINT N$;
360   IF INKEY$=""THEN 360
370 REM NOW PRINT Y LABEL VERTICALLY
380   FOR I=1 TO LEN(M$):M1$=MID$(M$,I,1)
390      MOVE 120,AY-((I-1)*16)
400   PRINT M1$;
410   NEXT I
412   MOVE 480,60:PRINT MX;
414   MOVE 130,382:PRINT MY;
420 REM NOW PLOT POINTS
430 FOR I=1 TO P
440   MOVE 194+(300*(X(I)/MX)),86+(300*(Y(I)/MY))
445      PRINT CHR$(231);
450 NEXT I
```

GRAPH is a little more complex than the programs we have considered so far, and its main sections are as follows:

For the first time this program introduces the notion of using *arrays* to hold data. You will find that this technique is one of the central methods of computer

graphics, and the uses of arrays are discussed at length in Chapter 3. The GRAPH program also illustrates the use of variables in a simple FOR NEXT loop to draw a series of lines. This is a valuable technique that works as follows. In the GRAPH program we wish to draw a series of marks along each axis. These marks could be laboriously drawn by a series of individual MOVE and DRAW instructions, but why do all the work when the computer can do it for you? Look at lines 210 to 240 of GRAPH, which control the marking of the Y axis. Line 170 sets the number of marks that are to be drawn: any number would be possible, within the resolution limits of the computer. Lines 220-230 contain the instructions to draw each mark. The start and finish X coordinates are 190 and 200 respectively. But instead of drawing the same mark a number of times we need to move down (or up) the Y axis for each new mark. The start and finish Y coordinates will be the same for each Y axis mark. Each successive pair of Y coordinates are set to a multiple of the FOR NEXT counter I: in this case the multiplier is 30. Because the marks are to be set at Y= 50,80,110 and so on rather than 0,30,60, a constant amount of 50 is added to each Y value. The same technique is used along the X axis in lines 250 to 280 of GRAPH.

1.6 Placement of text

There are in fact two methods which can be used to place text on the high resolution screen. As the text and graphics screens on Amstrad computers share the same location in memory, they can be accessed at the same time. This means that you can use the standard BASIC command

    PRINT "WHATEVER YOU LIKE"

to add text to a picture. The problem is that a bald statement of this kind will put the text at the current position of the text cursor, which will almost certainly be in the wrong place. To overcome this problem, Amstrad BASIC provides the LOCATE command. In the simplest case for example, the command

    LOCATE 10,20

puts the text cursor at the 10th column in the 20th row.

Unfortunately, LOCATE is of limited use for high resolution graphics. In order to make use of LOCATE to label a picture it is necesssary to transform the row, column start position (i.e. addressing a 40 * 25 area in MODE 1) to the 640 * 400 screen unit area. This can of course be done, because the size of each text cell is constant. It does involve needless calculation however. The solution is to use a new command called TAG. TAG allows the start position of the text string to be at a given pixel, so

```
TAG
MOVE 100,200
PRINT"WHATEVER YOU LIKE";
TAGOFF
```

will print the string starting at pixel 100,200. Note that **TAG** is a somewhat dangerous command, because all text will be 'tied' to the current graphics cursor position until the **TAGOFF** command is used. You may like to note (and may already know) that both **LOCATE** and **TAG** commands may be specified for particular output streams, and the use of streams will be discussed in section 7 below.

1.7 Printing graphics

Although the first goal of any graphics work is to produce the expected output from the program on screen, 'hard copy', either produced on a dot matrix printer or a pen plotter is both useful and rewarding. What options are open to the Amstrad computer owner? Amstrad produce a printer (the DMP 1) which can be used to output text and to print graphics.

The DMP 1 is one of the cheapest dot matrix printers around, and costs around £200 (August 1985). It prints the full Amstrad low resolution graphics set: useful if you want to use the low resolution graphics capabilities of your machine. The quality of the output is fairly low, and the DMP 1 uses only perforated paper as it has a tractor feed mechanism and has no friction feed for unperforated paper. The DMP 1 does allow a 'graphics dump' (i.e. a printing of all the pixels on screen) to be performed.

Now the beauty of the Amstrad computers is that they have a standard parallel Centronics interface. This means that any Centronics compatible printer can be connected by purchasing a cable (note that the socket on the back of the computer does not take a Centronics type connector, so you will have to buy a special cable for around £10-15).

By specifying stream eight in output commands, output can be directly written to the printer. Note that screen dumps cannot automatically be done, and special software will have to be used to perform this task. Recent issues of several computer magazines have included listings of programs to do screen dumps, and there are three classes of software for this purpose. Very much the worst performance is offered by screen dump programs written in BASIC - it may take up to half an hour to copy a single screen! Magazine listings using machine code are much quicker, but often have no facility for shading and may not be able to copy the full width of the screen.

The best solution is to buy one of the commercially available software packages. Such packages may be able to cope with the full screen width by printing screens vertically (long axis down the paper). The best package is probably Tascopy (Tasman Software Ltd). Tascopy allows production of screen copies in all screen modes, with full grey scale representation of colour (see for example Figures 1.6 and 1.11).

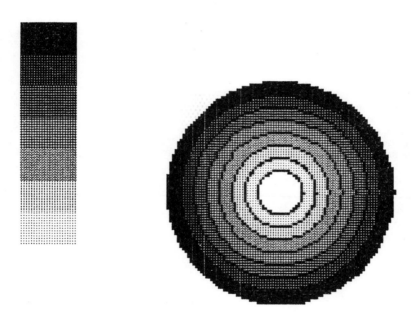

Figure 1.11 An example of colour shading using Tascopy

The grey shades can be specified by the user. Tascopy also allows you to make poster size screen copies on four sheets of printer paper (by drawing a quarter of the screen on each piece, the pieces subsequently being pasted together). A variety of printer types including the DMP 1 can be used with the package. All the screen dumps shown in this book have been obtained using Tascopy.

Assuming that you have a printer capable of copying the high resolution screen, you may find that the proportions of X and Y axes on the printer are different from those on the screen. To test this, try printing the output from the CIRCLE program above. Trial and error will show you how to compensate for the difference. Using a sophisticated package like Tascopy will obviate these problems.

The following short program (SCREEN) outlines the screen dimensions and you can use it to see the screen dump size and XY ratios available on your printer. You will of course need to include the correct screen dump command for the printer software that you are using.

SCREEN program

```
10 REM ****PROGRAM SCREEN****
15 CLS
20 MOVE 1,1
30 DRAW 639,1
40 DRAW 639,399
50 DRAW 1,399
60 DRAW 1,1
70 REM NOW DRAW CROSS AT CENTRE
80 MOVE 310,200
90 DRAW 330,200
100 MOVE 320,190
110 DRAW 320,210
```

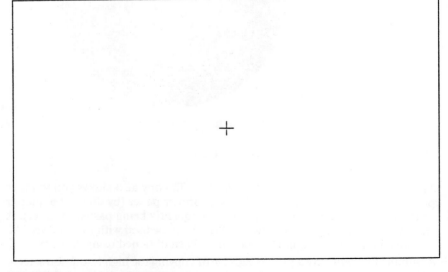

Figure 1.12 Output from SCREEN

34

This chapter has demonstrated the use of the Amstrad computers to produce graphics images, but we have not yet looked in a logical fashion at the commands used to create graphics on the screen. We will investigate these commands in Chapter 2.

Chapter 2
Points, Lines and Shapes

2.1 Drawing lines

We have already seen some simple graphics programs in Chapter 1, but no explanation of the various graphics commands has yet been given. Appendix 1 lists the graphics commands that are used on the CPC 6128, 664 and 464, and in this chapter we will build up an armoury of the more common commands used in the rest of the book. Let us begin with the simplest 'graphics primitives': points and lines.

To start with we will not concern ourselves with streams or ink colours. Suppose we wish to draw a line from point X1,Y1 to point X2,Y2. To do this on an Amstrad computer the following commands would be used

```
MOVE X1,Y1
DRAW X2,Y2
```

The current position of the 'graphics cursor' will move to the point specified by the last graphics command. After the above two statements it will therefore be at position X2,Y2. Recall that MOVE and DRAW instructions were used for the graphics programs in Chapter 1.

At the start of a graphics programming session, the graphics cursor will be at position 0,0 - the bottom left hand corner of the screen. This point is termed the origin. Amstrad BASIC has an additional command called appropriately enough ORIGIN which allows you to move the origin anywhere within the screen area. The line drawn above could therefore be drawn using the ORIGIN command thus

```
ORIGIN X1,Y1
DRAW X2,Y2
```

Use of ORIGIN allows you to specify *negative* coordinates! If you try to plot the following line

```
DRAW -10,-10
```

You will obtain a single dot at position 0,0 because all the other points from the 0,0 origin to position -10,-10 are off the screen. If you instead use

```
DRAW -10,-10 ORIGIN -100,100
```

a line will in fact be drawn, because the true endpoint of the line is at position 90,90.

Up until now we have been concerned with drawing lines, but it is often necessary to erase lines, either because they have been drawn in the wrong place, or because the picture is to be updated (rotated, for example). The usual way of doing this is to include an extra parameter in the DRAW command which defines what is to be done to each pixel along the line. You will find this extra parameter referred to as the 'ink mode' in your User Manual, and four ink modes are available. These modes are

0   Plot normally
1   Perform an eXclusive OR (XOR) on each pixel
2   Perform an AND on each pixel
3   Perform an OR on each pixel

The ink mode defaults to 0 if you do not specify a mode, so each pixel is normally lit. Use of ink mode 1 is especially useful as it allows you to 'wipe out' lit pixels

The following short program demonstrates the use of this erase facility by drawing lines at random on the screen and immediately wiping them off again.

NOWYOUSEEIT program

```
10 REM ****PROGRAM NOWYOUSEEIT****
20 RANDOMIZE
30 CLS
40 X1=RND(1)*640:REM SET FIRST X VAL
50 Y1=RND(1)*400:REM SET FIRST Y VAL
60 X2=RND(1)*640:REM SET SECOND X VAL
70 Y2=RND(1)*400:REM SET SECOND Y VAL
80 MOVE X1,Y1
90 DRAW X2,Y2
100 REM NOW WIPE LINE
110 REM INK MODE 1 (XOR) WILL WIPE EXISTING LINE
120 MOVE X1,Y1,1,1
130 DRAW X2,Y2,1,1
140 GOTO 40
```

By specifying ink mode 1 you can 'invert' pixels (ie turn them on if they are off or turn them off if they are on). Inversion has two main uses. Its first, less formal role is in the drawing of pretty patterns. Program INVERT below shows the ability of inversion to generate complex and striking patterns with little programming effort.

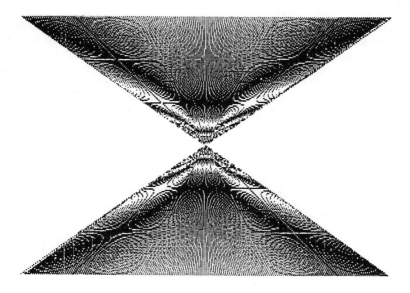

Figure 2.1 Output from INVERT

INVERT program

```
10 REM ****PROGRAM INVERT****
15 CLS
17 N=0
20 X1=40:Y1=0
30 X2=600:Y2=400
40 X1=X1+3:X2=X2-3
50 IF X1>600 THEN X1=41:N=N+1
60 IF X2<40 THEN X2=599
70 MOVE X1,Y1,1,1
80 DRAW X2,Y2,1,1
83 IF N=1 THEN N=2
85 IF X1=41 THEN INK 1,N
90 GOTO 40
```

The more utilitarian value of the inversion technique is in preventing picture element erasure when overwriting part of the picture. We will use inversion in Chapter 3 to prevent wiping of a picture by a cursor moving over it. Consider a line extending vertically halfway across the screen. If an object is moved across the screen by erasing it at, say, location X1, and redrawing it at location X2, then when the object crosses the vertical line the erasure command will erase any pixel on the line which overlaps the object to be erased. If however, inversion is used rather than erasure, the object will still disappear when required to (because all lit pixels become inverted, i.e. they become unlit). How does this affect the vertical line? When the object reaches the line, inversion turns off the pixels on the line which overlap the object, and when this object position is later inverted (to turn off the object) the vertical line is 'made new' again as re-inversion occurs. This process is shown pictorially in Figure 2.2

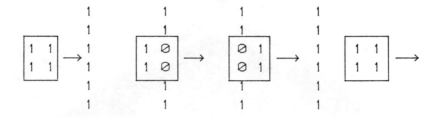

Figure 2.2 The inversion technique in action. The sequence of frames shows the movement of a square object across a vertical line, without permanently erasing any line pixel. As the pixels in the square and line meet, they are inverted, and are turned off (that is, 1 + 1 = 0). When the square leaves the vertical line, inverting the pixels vacated by the square turns on the line pixels again.

2.2 Points

So far we have only considered lines, but it is often necessary to plot individual pixels. Amstrad BASIC uses the PLOT command to do this job, and the command is used in a similar way to DRAW. To plot a single pixel at position X1,Y1

```
PLOT X1,Y1
```

and to draw a horizontal dotted line across the screen

```
MOVE 100,100
FOR X=100 TO 600 STEP 10
PLOT X,100
NEXT X
```

Plotting points rather than lines can also be very useful if you want to check if two lines intersect. You may wish to draw a line that does not cross another line for example. Try the following short program

JOIN program

```
10 REM **** PROGRAM JOIN ****
20 REM DEMONSTRATES USE OF TEST COMMAND
30 CLS
40 INK 0,13:INK 1,0
50    MOVE 300,300
60    DRAW 300,100
70       FOR X=0 TO 640
80       IF TEST(X,200)<>0 THEN 200
90       PLOT X,200
100      NEXT X
200 STOP
```

This program draws a vertical line and then constructs a horizontal line by plotting adjacent pixels. The command $TEST(X,Y)$ checks if the pixel at position X,Y to be lit along the horizontal line is in fact already lit. When the horizontal line reaches the vertical line this condition is true, so the program stops.

2.3 Drawing shapes

You saw in the last chapter that repetitive use of the $DRAW$ command allows shapes to be built up. You may wish to experiment by drawing an outline on graph paper marked out in a 640 * 400 unit box. Your shape can be drawn on the computer by specifying a $DRAW$ instruction for each adjacent point on the outline. Remember to use a $MOVE$ command to move to the first point of your outline, or you will have an ugly extra line from the origin to the first point. You will need extra $MOVE$ commands if you have disconnected parts of your outline.

2.4 Dashes and fills

The lucky CPC 6128 or CPC 664 owner has several commands in his or her graphics armoury that are not available to the CPC464 buff. In particular the **MASK** command allows various dash patterns to be drawn instead of an unbroken line. This command is of the form

    MASK number

where 'number' is an integer number between 0 and 255. **MASK** sets pixels in each adjacent group of 8 to OFF (0) or ON (1). The following program displays some typical patterns on the screen, but please remember that it is for the CPC664 only.

Figure 2.3 Output from MASKDEMO

MASKDEMO program

```
10 REM **** MASK DEMO PROGRAM ****
15 MODE 1
20 CLS
25 LOCATE 5,2:PRINT"EXAMPLES OF MASK VALUES"
27 LOCATE 5,4:PRINT"MODE = 1"
30 Y=300
40 DATA 1,3,33,7,15,31,63,127
50 FOR I=1 TO 8
60    READ M
70    MASK M
80    Y=Y-30
90    MOVE 100,Y
100   DRAW 400,Y
110   TAG
120 PRINT M;
140 NEXT I
```

In order to use **MASK** effectively you will need to remember (or learn, shame on you) some elementary binary numbering. Recall that binary 255 is represented by

1 1 1 1 1 1 1 1

and that binary 0 is represented by

0 0 0 0 0 0 0 0

so if you specify a MASK of 255, a solid line results, while a **MASK** of 0 produces no line. If you wanted to plot each alternate pixel you would use one of the following **MASKS**

1 0 1 0 1 0 1 0

or

0 1 0 1 0 1 0 1

represented by the decimal numbers 170 and 85 respectively.

If you do not have a CPC 6128/664, all is not lost. The following program will allow you to plot a line between two points using a dashed pattern.

DASH program

```
10 REM FOR CPC 464 OWNERS WITHOUT MASK COMMAND
20 REM DRAWS DASHED LINE FROM X1,Y1 TO X2,Y2
30    CLS
40    INPUT"INCREMENT?";INCREMENT
50    GOSUB 240:REM GET END POINTS
60      MOVE X1,Y1
70 REM FIRST CALCULATE LENGTH OF THE LINE
80    HY2=(X2-X1)^2 + (Y2-Y1)^2
90    HY =SQR(HY2)
100      INC=INCREMENT*(HY/300)
110      PLOT X1,Y1,1,0
120      PLOT X2,Y2,1,0
130 REM NOW FIND RATIOS FOR X AND Y INCREMENTS
140    XR=(X2-X1)/INC:YR=(Y2-Y1)/INC
150 REM NOW DRAW THE LINE
160    DASH=0
170      FOR I=1 TO INC
180        IF DASH=0 THEN DASH=2:GOTO 200
190        IF DASH=2 THEN DASH=0
200        X1=X1+XR:Y1=Y1+YR
210        DRAW X1,Y1,1,DASH
220      NEXT I
230    GOSUB 240:GOTO 60
240 REM RANDOM END POINT ROUTINE
250    X1=RND(1)*600:X2=RND(1)*600
260    Y1=RND(1)*400:Y2=RND(1)*400
270 RETURN
```

INCREMENT?? 20

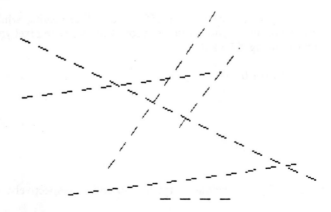

Figure 2.4

44

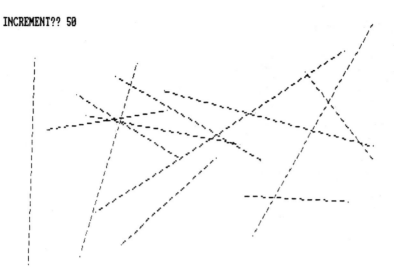

Figure 2.4,2.5 Two examples of output from the DASH program

Perhaps a more serious shortcoming of the CPC464 is the lack of the F I L L command on this machine. F I L L merely fills a space FROM THE CURRENT GRAPHICS CURSOR POSITION with a chosen ink colour. The form of the command is simply

> FILL ink number

The FILL operation only stops when lit pixels are reached, so if you try to fill a space that is not completely bounded by lit pixels beware: the whole screen area may become filled! I cannot offer a full F I L L simulation for the CPC464 owner in this book, but you will find a program called PATTERN in Chapter 5 that will allow you to fill rectangular areas (for example in bar charts) with various hatched patterns.

2.5 Drawing curves

We saw how to draw a circle in Chapter 1, and it is often useful to be able to construct other curved shapes. First, let us consider an ellipse. The equations to be used are almost identical to those used for a circle, but different radii are used for the X and Y axes. Try this version of the CIRCLE program (we now call it ELLIPSE) for different values of RX and RY.

ELLIPSE program

```
10 REM ****PROGRAM ELLIPSE****
20 REM TO CONSTRUCT CIRCLE FROM CALCULATED COORDINATES
30 INK 0,0
40 INK 1,12
50 MODE 1
60 PAPER 0
70 GRAPHICS PEN 1:REM LINES 30-70 SET UP DRAWING COLOURS
80 INPUT"X,Y RADII?";XR,YR
90 AN=0
100 AI=0.062831853
110 X1=XR*COS(AN):Y1=YR*SIN(AN)
120 FOR I=1 TO 100
130 X=X1:Y=Y1
140 AN=AN+AI
150 X1=XR*COS(AN):Y1=YR*SIN(AN)
160 MOVE X+320,Y+200
170 DRAW X1+320,Y1+200
180 NEXT I
190 END
```

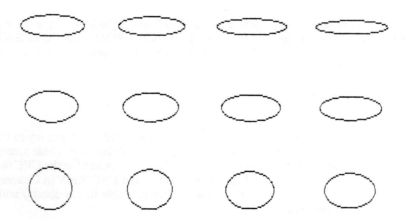

Figure 2.6 Ellipses for various values of RX and RY drawn using the ELLIPSE program

The general equation for a sine curve can be written as

$$Y = H * SIN (W * X + D)$$

46

where W is the frequency (determining the number of oscillations) for a given range of X. D specifies the curve's right (positive) or left (negative) displacement. Here is a program for generating sine curves

SINE program

```
10 REM **** PROGRAM SINEWAVE ****
20 CLS
30 INK 0,13:INK 1,0
40    INPUT"MAX Y VALUE?";YV
45    M=YV/2
50    INPUT"H,W,D";H,W,D:REM USE 40,.1,0 TO TEST
60    IF H>M THEN 40
70    INPUT"XMIN,XMAX";XMIN,XMAX
80       YA=H*SIN(W*XMIN+D)
90       IF YA>=0 THEN YA=M-YA
100      IF YA<0  THEN YA=M+ABS(YA)
110      XA=XMIN
120        FOR XB=XMIN TO XMAX
130        YB=H*SIN(W*XB+D)
140        IF YB>=0 THEN YB=M-YB
150        IF YB<0  THEN YB=M+ABS(YB)
160          MOVE XA,YA
170          DRAW XB,YB
180          XA=XB
190          YA=YB
200        NEXT XB
210 END
```

SINE CURVE: H=175,W=.05,D=0

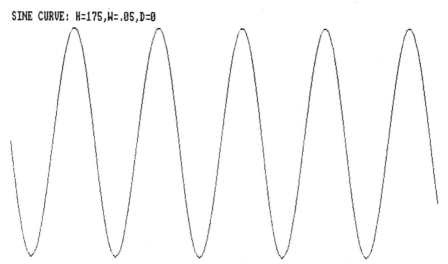

Figure 2.7 A sine curve drawn using the SINE program

47

A parabola is a useful curve that can be used to describe the motion of objects. The equation to calculate a Y coordinate is

$$Y = C1 * X^2 + C2 * X + C3$$

where C1, C2 and C3 are three coefficients that can be varied to produce different parabolic trajectories. Program PARA draws a parabolic curve after input of the maximum X and Y values, together with values for C1,C2 and C3. Try varying these coefficients! The parabola will be at a maximum at the centre if C1>0.

PARA program

```
10 REM **** PROGRAM PARA ****
20 REM DRAWS A PARABOLA
25 DIM C(3)
30 CLS:MODE 2
40   INK 0,13:INK 1,0
50   INPUT"MAX X AND Y VALUES";MX,MY
60   INPUT"C1,C2,C3";C(1),C(2),C(3)
70   XC=320
80     X=-C(2)/(2*C(1))
90     YV=C(1)*X^2+C(2)*X+C(3)
100    IF C(1)<0 THEN YA=0
110    IF C(1)>0 THEN YA=MY
120     XL1=320:XL2=320:XR1=320:XR2=320
130     X=X-1
140     N=3
150     Y=C(1)
160     FOR I=2 TO N
170       Y=Y*X+C(I)
175     NEXT I
180       IF C(1)<0 THEN YB=YV-Y
190       IF C(1)>0 THEN YB=MY-(Y-YV)
200       XL2=XL2-1
210       XR2=XR2+1
220       MOVE XL1,YA
230       DRAW XL2,YB
240       MOVE XR1,YA
250       DRAW XR2,YB
260     YA=YB
270     XL1=XL2
280     XR1=XR2
285     IF YA<1 THEN 300
290     GOTO 130
300     C(1)=C(1)+0.005:C(2)=C(2)+0.005:C(3)=C(3)+0.005
310 GOTO 80
```

```
MAX X AND Y VALUES? 360,300
C1,C2,C3? .004,.004,.004
```

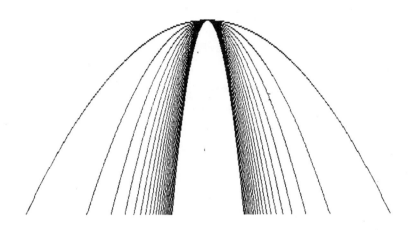

Figure 2.8 A group of parabolas drawn using the PARA program

2.6 Vector animation

Graphic lines are sometimes called 'vectors', and animation of lines is usually termed 'vector animation'. If you wish to animate line drawings you will find it rather frustrating to program in BASIC. The reason is that even the rather quick Amstrad BASIC cannot wipe and redraw more than a minimum of lines without flicker. Type in the following short program that moves an 'arrowhead' across the screen. Try varying the size of the arrow and the step size taken. You will find that the larger the arrow, the slower the movement.

VECTOR program

```
10 REM VECTOR ANIMATION PROGRAM
20 REM MOVES AN 'ARROW' ACROSS THE SCREEN
30   INK 0,13:INK 1,0
35   INPUT "ARROW LENGTH?";N
37   INPUT "STEP SIZE";M
40 MODE 2
50   FOR X=1 TO 640 STEP M
```

```
55       GOSUB 100:REM WIPE ARROW
57 FRAME
60       GOSUB 200:REM DRAW ARROW
70     NEXT X
80 END
100 REM SUBROUTINE TO WIPE ARROW
110    MOVE X,200
120    DRAW X+N,190,1,1
130    DRAW X,180,1,1
140    DRAW X,200,1,1
150 RETURN
200 REM SUBROUTINE TO DRAW AND WIPE ARROW
210    MOVE X,200
220    DRAW X+N,190
230    DRAW X,180
240    DRAW X,200
250 RETURN
```

You can see that the program uses the **FRAME** command to synchronize line drawing with the screen refresh. Try running the program without **FRAME** and you will see a noticeable drop in picture quality.

Note that this vector drawing program uses the 'Xor' ink mode to wipe out the existing image before drawing a new image further across the screen.

2.7 Fractals

We will conclude this short chapter with a little 'light recreation': light at least in the aesthetic nature of the pictures that you can produce. Fractal geometry is a specialized form of geometry which deals not with one, two or three dimensions, but with the 'no-mans-land' between these dimensions. You have probably seen the beautiful three dimensional mountain ranges and forest-scapes produced by leading exponents of mainframe computer graphics, notably the 'Star Wars', LucasFilm team: these pictures are made up of fractal curves, and although the mathematics and computer processing power required to produce such artwork are quite beyond the scope of this book, you can use a little arithmetic and a simple pixel plotting instruction to generate your own fractals with dimensions between one and two.

The following program is a modification of one by Greg Turk. In mathematical terms, the type of fractal generated by this program results from the behaviour of points in the plane described by the function $x + iy$, where x and y are real numbers and i is the square root of -1. The effect shown in the program output

(Figure 1.15) is produced by iteration: solving the function repeatedly for each current value of x and y. To get the x and y points from the function, you need to work out the following equations:

new pt x = LA * old X * (1-X)
new pt y = LA * old Y * (1-Y)

LA is a constant in the equation. You can experiment with LA to get different fractal curves. You can also adjust the size of the picture by varying SC S C=2 for the plots in Figure 2.9). The smaller SC, the quicker the picture will be drawn. Be prepared to wait ten or fifteen minutes though: this program does a lot of number crunching.

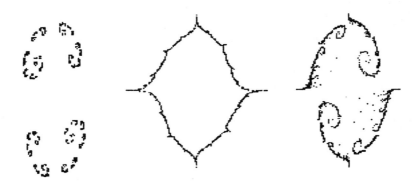

Figure 2.9 Fractal curves of between one and two dimensions obtained using FRACTAL.

FRACTAL program

```
10 REM ****PROGRAM FRACTAL****
20 REM DEMONSTRATES POINT PLOTTING TO PRODUCE ABSTRACT SHAPES
30 RANDOMIZE
40 MODE 1
50 INK 0,0:INK 1,24
60 CX=320:CY=200
70 X=0.50001:Y=0
```

```
80 GOSUB 390
90 FOR I=1 TO 10:GOSUB 310:NEXT I
100 GOSUB 460
110 GOSUB 310
120 GOTO 100
130 END
140 REM SQUARE ROOT OF X,Y
150 T=Y
160 S=SQR(ABS(X*X+Y*Y))
170 Y=SQR(ABS((-X+S)/2))
180 X=SQR(ABS((X+S)/2))
190 IF T<O THEN X=-X
200 RETURN
210 REM FOUR OVER L
220 S=LX*LX+LY*LY
230 LX=4*LX/S
240 LY=-4*LY/S
250 RETURN
260 REM X,Y TIMES L
270 TX=X:TY=Y
280 X=TX*LX-TY*LY
290 X=TX*LX-TY*LY
300 RETURN
310 REM FUNCTION OF X,Y
320 GOSUB 260
330 X=1-X
340 GOSUB 140
350 IF RND(1)<0.5 THEN X=-X:Y=-Y
360 X=1-X
370 X=X/2:Y=Y/2
380 RETURN
390 REM GET VALUES
400 INPUT "LAMBDA VALUE?";LX,LY
410 GOSUB 210
420 INPUT "SCALE VALUE";SC
430 SC=2*CX/SC
440 CLS
450 RETURN
460 REM PLOT X,Y
470 PLOT SC*(X-0.5)+CX,CY-SC*Y
480 RETURN
```

Chapter Three
Graphics Data Structures

3.1 Input of data

We have already seen that any point on the screen can be defined by its x,y coordinates. Plotting a single point or drawing a line is therefore extremely simple. Plotting a small number of joined points is also easy, but what if we wish to draw a complex figure that has 50 or even 100 lines, not all of which are joined in one sequential length?

A standard procedure for both inputting and for holding data is therefore necessary, and must specify three things

(1)   The x,y locations of all the points in the figure.
(2)   The ordering of the points (ie the order in which they are to be plotted).
(3)   The connection between the points (are two consecutive points to be joined or not?)

Study of computer data structures makes up a significant part of an honours degree in computer science, and although advanced graphics techniques rely heavily on complex data structures, we will limit ourselves to the array structure. This is, in many ways, the most rudimentary of data structures, but as none of the others are supported in BASIC our choice is not a free one!

We first take two one-dimensional arrays $X(1 .. n)$, $Y(1 .. n)$, where n is the total number of points to be drawn. Of course, both X and Y must be dimensioned the same, as each point has both x and y coordinates. We will call these arrays the coordinate data. As $X(1)$ precedes $X(2)$, these arrays also allow the ordering of the data: point $X(1),Y(1)$ is drawn before $X(2),Y(2)$ and so on.

Next, the connections between the points must be considered. This information is provided by a third array, this time a two dimensional one. The line array is dimensioned $W(1 .. 2,1 .. i)$ where i is the number of lines to be drawn in the picture. Now the first dimension of the array W indicates that for each line number there are two items of data, as you can see in the next table. These two items of data are not coordinates as such but are what are termed indices (sing. index). An index in computer jargon is merely a pointer to some other piece of information in the computer. In this case each index points to an element number in the X and Y arrays. The first index for each line corresponds to the coordinates of the start point for the line. The second index corresponds to the finish point for the line. So the complete data for drawing a square might look as follows.

i	XX(i)	Y(i)	W(1,i)	W(2,i)
1	50	150	1	2
2	150	150	2	3
3	150	50	3	4
4	50	50	4	1

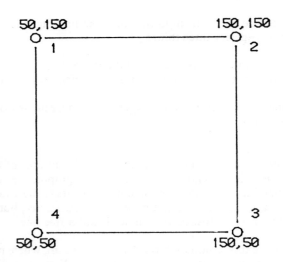

Figure 3.1 Points and coordinates for a square

Notice that the number of points in X, Y and W are the same in this example, but this need not always be the case. If the following picture is to be drawn, the W array would contain a break as you can see from the data under the picture

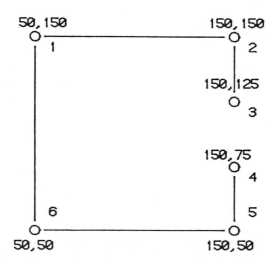

Figure 3.2 Points and coordinates for a square with a 'break'

i	X(i)	Y(i)	W(1,i)	W(2,i)
1	50	150	1	2
2	150	150	2	3
3	150	125	4	5
4	150	75	5	6
5	150	50	6	1
6	50	150		

The following program section would read in the data for this rectangle and would then plot it. Note the two variables NPTS and LI. These just specify the number of points and the number of lines respectively. We will use these variables throughout this book.

EASYDRAW program

```
10 REM ****PROGRAM EASYDRAW****
20 REM DEMONSTRATES POINT AND LINE DRAWING FROM DATA IN STORED ARRAYS
30 CLS
40 REM SET UP POINT ARRAY
50 READ NPTS
```

```
60 DIM X(NPTS),Y(NPTS)
70 FOR I=1 TO NPTS
80 READ X(I),Y(I)
90 NEXT I
100 READ LI
110 DIM LN(2,LI)
120 FOR I=1 TO LI
130 READ LN(1,I),LN(2,I)
140 NEXT I
150 REM NOW DRAW THE PICTURE
160 FOR I=1 TO LI
170 MOVE X(LN(1,I)),Y(LN(1,I))
180 DRAW X(LN(2,I)),Y(LN(2,I))
190 NEXT I
200 STOP
210 DATA 6,100,100,300,100,300,150,300,250,300,300,100,300
220 DATA 5,1,2,2,3,4,5,5,6,6,1
```

By using the X, Y and W arrays to store the picture information, you can construct any line drawing you wish. You can also use differently coloured lines, so long as they are not in the same 8 X 8 bit character block. This form of data input by data statements in lines of the program is less than ideal because it means you have to change the program every time a new set of data is to be used. This is trivial for a ten line program like the one listed above, but what about input to a piece of professional software that is both read and write protected? The best solution is to use a sequential file to hold the data needed to draw the picture. We must therefore (1) write a short program to create the data file and (2) amend our drawing program(s) to access data from the sequential files created.

The program FILE2D below allows you to enter the X, Y and W array data into a sequential file. The program starts by asking for the sequential file name you wish to use.

Now the program sections to read and write from sequential files will be the same for all the three Amstrad computers. It is of little interest to Amstrad BASIC whether you have a disk drive or a tape drive - your machine will default to whichever is connected. In this book we will restrict ourselves to the following simple input/output commands

```
OPENIN "FILENAME*
INPUT#9, VARIABLES
CLOSEIN

OPENOUT "FILENAME"
PRINT#9, VARIABLES
CLOSEOUT
```

A word of warning for disk users - if a sequential file with the same name already exists it will be overwritten! Amstrad BASIC gives you a degree of safety in that the existing file is saved under the name FILENAME.BAK. If a third version of the same file is saved, however, the version in FILENAME.BAK will be lost as it will be overwritten by the second backup version.

FILE2D program

```
10 REM ****PROGRAM FILE2D
20 REM PROGRAM TO STORE COORDINATE DATA TO BE DRAWN USING DRAW2D
30 INPUT"FILENAME?";H$
40 OPENOUT H$
50 INPUT"NUMBER OF POINTS?";NPTS
55 WRITE£9,NPTS
60 PRINT"ENTER X,Y PAIRS"
70 FOR I=1 TO NPTS
80 INPUT"X=";X:INPUT"Y=";Y
90 WRITE£9,X
100 WRITE£9,Y
110 NEXT I
120 INPUT"NUMBER OF LINES?";LI
130 WRITE£9,LI
140 PRINT"ENTER NUMBERS OF JOINING POINTS"
150 FOR I=1 TO LI
160 INPUT"START NO";SN:INPUT"FINISH NO";FI
170 WRITE£9,SN
180 WRITE£9,FI
190 NEXT I
200 CLOSEOUT
210 END
```

Note that FILE2D does not need to concern itself with data structures at all because its sole role in life is to transfer a sequence of numbers to a disk or tape file. The program to draw a picture from the data in a sequential file created using FILE2D is listed below. As you can see, this program (DRAW2D) is the 'reverse' of FILE2D as it 'plucks back' the relevent data to fill the X, Y and W arrays. These three arrays are dimensioned in accordance with the values of the variables NPTS and LI in the sequential file

DRAW2D program

```
10 REM ****PROGRAM DRAW2D****
20 REM DRAWS IMAGE FROM DATA HELD IN FILE2D FORMAT
30 INPUT"FILENAME?";H$
```

```
40 OPENIN H$
50 REM SET UP POINT ARRAYS
60 INPUT£9,NPTS
70 DIM X(NPTS),Y(NPTS)
80 FOR I=1 TO NPTS
90 INPUT£9,X(I):INPUT£9,Y(I)
100 NEXT I
110 INPUT£9,LI
120 REM SET UP LINE ARRAY
130 DIM LN(2,LI)
140 FOR I=1 TO LI
150 INPUT£9,LN(1,I),LN(2,I)
160 NEXT I
170 CLOSEIN
180 REM NOW DRAW THE PICTURE
190 CLS
200 FOR I=1 TO LI
210 MOVE X(LN(1,I)),Y(LN(1,I))
220 DRAW X(LN(2,I)),Y(LN(2,I))
230 NEXT I
240 END
```

The only tricky bit of programming in DRAW2D can be found in lines 210-220 which do the actual drawing on screen. As drawing is done between pairs of X,Y coordinates, it follows that the X and Y coordinates must be given in this program line. However, we really want to be able to specify the series of **LINES** which are to be drawn. We have already seen that the indices of the start and finish **POINTS** for each line i are given by W(1,i) and W(2,i). It therefore follows that the array element X(W(1,i)) is the X coordinate of the start point of line 1, and X(W(2,i)) is the X coordinate of the finish point of the same line. The **FOR NEXT** loop between lines 200-230 sequentially draws all the lines in the picture by accessing the X and Y coordinates via the X and Y array indices 'pointed to' by the elements of the W array.

3.2 More complex data sets

How many dimensions?

In the simplest cases that we have looked at so far, there has been a direct equivalence between the coordinate data from our data file, and the coordinates plotted on the screen. With two dimensional data this one to one correspondence is often possible to achieve, although some kind of 'scaling' operation to fit data to the screen may be necessary - we will look at how to handle this in the next chapter. Three dimensional data needs special care: the data is defined in terms of X, Y and Z coordinates, but as the screen is only two dimensional, we have to 'lose' the third dimension again. We will see how to carry out this kind of transformation in Chapter 7. For the moment, we merely need to note that the Z data is provided in the form of a third one dimensional array to join its X and Y companions.

Picture segments

More important at this stage is the possible modular nature of the picture that we wish to draw. If you consider a screen full of information as a single entity constructed of information derived from the X, Y and W arrays, then it is a static set of data which may be very aesthetic to look at, but is restricted in its usefulness. What happens if we want to interact with the picture in some way? Perhaps we wish to move part of the picture to a different location on the screen, or alternatively we may want to erase or amend part of the picture.

In order to consider parts of the picture without the whole, we must introduce a new concept, the segment. A picture segment is a section of a picture which may be treated in its own right.

If the total picture is to be treated as one segment, then our X, Y and W arrays are quite sufficient to store and construct the segment. If more than one segment is to be displayed, the input data must be stored in either a series of arrays (X1, Y1, Z1 ... Xn, Yn, Zn), or else the segments can be stored as blocks in the single X, Y and Z arrays. This latter method is neater and more widely used, so this is the one for us. So what method do we use to define the segments if they are all in one array? Let us take a pictorial example first.

The diagram shows a simple scene built up of four different segments, a table, four chairs, a television set and a lamp. We will assume that this framework is part of a 'room layout' design program, where the observer can move elements around the screen at will.

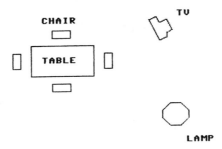

Figure 3.3 A scene built up of segments

59

The storage arrays for the data making up the segments might appear something like this:

i	X(i)	Y(i)	W(1,i)	W(2,i)
6 -10		TABLE	DATA	
11 -19		LAMP	DATA	
20 -28		TV	DATA	

Note that there is only one set of chair data, but four chairs are present in the picture. The ability to recall the segment data at will to copy individual segments demonstrates another aspect of their power. In order to access the data representing a particular segment, the start and finish indices for the segment are needed. In other words, we need to know the start point for the first line of each segment, for example the chair, and the finish point for the last line of the segment. To do this we define a new two dimensional array, which is dimensioned S (2 , N S), the N S representing the total number of segments, in this case four. The appearance of the S array for our room example is as follows:

i	S(1,i)	S(2,i)
1	1	6
2	7	11
3	12	20
4	21	29

So S(1,i) is the index of the start line for the ith segment and S(2,i) is the index of the finish line for the ith segment. You can see that our data structures are getting quite hairy now! We have a 'three tiered' system, with S array pointing to W array pointing to X and Y arrays.

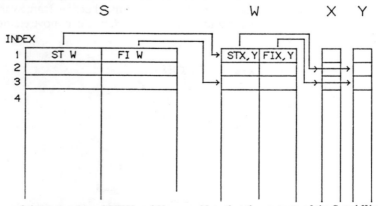

Figure 3.4 Relationship of S,W,X and Y arrays. Note that the contents of the S and W arrays are indices to the locations on the arrays to which they point. STX,Y = start coordinates of line. FIX,Y = end coordinates of line.

We now have all the information necessary to access the segment from the main program generating the picture.

3.3 Manipulating segments

You will not be able to harness the real power of segments until you have learned how to manipulate (ie move around and scale) picture elements, and a description of these manipulations makes up the bulk of Chapter 4. In order to display segments at varying places on the screen, for example, the technique of translation is used. You may however like to construct your own simple 'segmented' picture at this stage, and the following short sections of code can be added to FILE2D and DRAW2D respectively. These amendments in fact allow you to do little more than the programs without the additions but they do allow you to see how the S array is defined and used in an elementary way.

```
200  REM ADDITIONS TO FILE2D
210  INPUT"SEGMENTS";SN
220  PRINT#9,SN
230  PRINT"READ IN S ARRAY DATA"
240  FOR I=1 TO SN
250  INPUT J,K,L
260  PRINT#9,J:PRINT#9,K:PRINT#9,L
270  NEXT I
280  CLOSEOUT:END

240  REM ADDITIONS TO DRAW2D
250  INPUT#9,SN
260  DIM S(3,SN)
270  FOR I=1 TO SN
280  INPUT#9,S(1,I),S(2,I),S(3,I)
290  NEXT I
300  REM NOW DRAW A SEGMENT: CHANGE SEG TO DRAW OTHER
     SEGMENTS OTHER THAN NO 1
320  FOR I=S(1,SEG) TO S(2,SEG)
330  MOVE X(W(1,I)),Y(W(1,I))
340  DRAW X(W(2,I)),Y(W(2,I))
350  NEXT I
360  END
```

NOTE - All the program sections to be inserted in existing programs should overwrite existing line numbers if there is an overlap. Unless otherwise specified, all non-overlapping lines in both original program and insert are to be included in the new version of the program. The easiest way to do this is to (1) create a tape or disk file containing the additions, (2) load the original program into memory and finally (3) MERGE the additions into the main program.

3.4 Drawing pictures the easy way

So far we have seen how to produce a data set to represent single and multiple segments. The problem is of course that the data points have to be laboriously calculated by hand. There must be a better method! In this section we will look at a program which allows you to compose two dimensional data files at your leisure using screen and joystick. This program is called SKETCH after Sketchpad, the original of a similar name: one of the earliest computer aided design tools devised by Ivan Sutherland in the early 1960's.

SKETCH uses a joystick to move a cursor around the screen. The following actions control program flow.

Key pressed	Action
fire button	Initialise line
fire button	End line
B	Next point not joined
E	End segment
F	Finish picture
S	Start next segment

This control information is displayed on screen in the version of SKETCH given below. Once you have got used to the commands you will find it helpful to remove the GOSUB statement (line 135) to the text routine so that the instructions are not printed, as the bottom of the drawing area is covered by the instructions. You can see this from the following screen dump.

Once a line has been initialised, the cursor 'drags' the line from the start point around with it. This allows you to see the effect of placing a line in any given position. You may recall from our discussion of the pixel inversion technique at the end of the last chapter that this technique allows us to move parts of the picture over underlying picture elements without wiping out these elements and so you will find that all the LINE commands in SKETCH take the form of inversions rather than line draw/wipe instructions.

SKETCH is reproduced below. It is considerably longer than our other program examples so far, but you will find its use will save you more time in creating data files than you will expend in typing it into your computer.

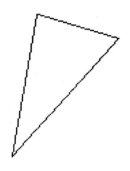

FIRE=START/FINISH LINE B=BREAK LINE
F=FINISH S=NEXT SEG E=END SEG

Figure 3.5 Screen dump of the SKETCH screen. A triangle has been drawn using the joystick

SKETCH program

```
5 REM ****PROGRAM SKETCH****
10 REM SET CURSOR AND STEP SIZES
20 CS=2:SS=2                      ' '
40 INPUT "DATA FILE NAME?";N$
45 CLS
50 REM NOW SET COUNTERS AND FLAGS
60 FL=0:NPTS=1:NA=1
70 LB=0:REM LINES COUNTER
80 SE=0:REM FLAG FOR SEGMENT END
90 S1=0:REM SEGMENT COUNTER
92 FI=0:REM FLAG FOR LINE BREAK
93 LI=0:REM SEGMENT LINE COUNTER
94 JY=1:REM LINE START/FINISH FLAG
100 DIM XP(500),YP(500),LN(2,500),S(3,10):REM DIMENSION ARRAYS
120 REM SET CURSOR IN CENTRE POSITION
130 X=320:Y=200
135     GOSUB 3500:REM PUT TEXT ON SCREEN
140     GOSUB 180:REM CURSOR PLOT ROUTINE
150     GOSUB 230:REM CURSOR MOVE ROUTINE
160     GOSUB 340:REM LINE DRAG ROUTINE
170 GOTO 140
```

```
180 REM CURSOR PLOT ROUTINE
190 X1=X-CS:Y1=Y-CS:X2=X+CS:Y2=Y+CS
200     MOVE X1,Y
205     DRAW X2,Y,1,1
210     MOVE X,Y1
215     DRAW X,Y2,1,1
220 RETURN
230 REM CURSOR MOVE ROUTINE
240 Y3=Y:X3=X
250     IF JOY(0)=0 THEN 310
260     IF JOY(0)=1 THEN Y=Y+SS:GOTO 310
270     IF JOY(0)=2 THEN Y=Y-SS:GOTO 310
280     IF JOY(0)=4 THEN X=X-SS:GOTO 310
290     IF JOY(0)=8 THEN X=X+SS:GOTO 310
310         MOVE X3,Y2
320         DRAW X3,Y1,1,1
325         MOVE X1,Y3
326         DRAW X2,Y3,1,1
330 RETURN
340 REM LINE DRAG AND PLOT ROUTINE
350 A$=INKEY$
355 IF A$=""AND JOY(0)<>16 THEN IF FL=0 THEN RETURN
370 IF JOY(0)=16 AND JY=1 THEN JY=2:LOCATE 1,1:PRINT"S":GOSUB 3000:GOTO 430
380 IF JOY(0)=16 AND JY=2 THEN JY=1:LOCATE 1,1:PRINT"F":GOSUB 3000:GOTO 460
390 IF A$="B"THEN JY=1:GOTO 450:REM BREAK LINE
400 IF A$="E"THEN SE=1:JY=1:GOTO 460:REM FINISH PICTURE
410 IF FL=0 THEN RETURN
420 GOTO 650:REM NORMAL LINE DRAW/WIPE
430 XI=X:YI=Y:REM START COORDINATES
440 FL=1:RETURN
450 FI=1:REM FLAG FOR LINE BREAK
460 XF=X:YF=Y:REM PUT IN POINT
480     MOVE XI,YI
485     DRAW XF,YF
490 NPTS=NPTS+1:NA=NA+1:LI=LI+1:LB=LB+1:REM INCREMENT COUNTERS
500 XP(NA)=XF:YP(NA)=YF:REM PUT IN POINTS
510 XP(NA-1)=XI:YP(NA-1)=YI:REM PUT IN POINTS
560 LN(1,LB)=NA-1:REM PUT IN LINE INDICES
570 LN(2,LB)=NA
580 IF FI=1 THEN NA=NA+1:FI=0:REM INCREMENT IF BREAK FLAG SET
590 IF SE=1 THEN S1=S1+1:S(1,S1)=NPTS-LI:S(2,S1)=NPTS-1:S(3,S1)=0:GOTO 690
630 FL=0:RETURN
640 FL=0
650 REM DO LINE DRAW/WIPE
660     MOVE X,Y
665     DRAW XI,YI,1,1
670     MOVE X,Y
675     DRAW XI,YI,1,1
680 RETURN
690 REM CONTINUE
710 FOR I=S(1,S1) TO S(2,S1)
730     MOVE XP(LN(1,I)),YP(LN(1,I))
735     DRAW XP(LN(2,I)),YP(LN(2,I)),1,0
740 NEXT I
```

```
750 K$=INKEY$:LOCATE 1,2:PRINT"ANOTHER SEGMENT?"
755 IF K$=""THEN 750:REM ANOTHER SEGMENT?
757 LOCATE 1,2:PRINT"                        "
770 IF K$="F" THEN 800:REM NO, SO FINISH
780 LI=0:FL=0:SE=0:NA=NA+1:REM YES, SO SET COUNTERS
790 RETURN
800 REM NOW CREATE FILE CONTAINING DATA
810 OPENOUT N$
840 WRITE£9,NA
850 FOR I=1 TO NA
860 WRITE£9,XP(I)
870 WRITE£9,YP(I)
875 NEXT I
880 WRITE£9,LB
890 FOR I=1 TO LB
900   WRITE£9,LN(1,I)
910   WRITE£9,LN(2,I)
915 NEXT I
920   WRITE£9,S1
930 FOR I=1 TO S1
940   WRITE£9,S(1,I)
950   WRITE£9,S(2,I)
960   WRITE£9,S(3,I)
965 NEXT I
970 CLOSEOUT
980 END
3000 FOR I=1 TO 200:NEXT I:RETURN
3500 LOCATE 13,1:PRINT"SKETCH PROGRAM";
3510 LOCATE 1,24:PRINT" FIRE=START/FINISH LINE B=BREAK LINE"
3520 LOCATE 1,25:PRINT"    F=FINISH S=NEXT SEG E=END SEG"
3530 MOVE 0,50
3540 DRAW 640,50
3600 RETURN
```

SKETCH may be broken down as follows:

LINES   5- 130   SETUP SCREEN, CURSOR AND ARRAYS
         135   PUT INSTRUCTIONS ON SCREEN
         140- 170 MAIN LOOP
         180- 330 CURSOR PLOT AND MOVE ROUTINES
         340- 400 READ CONTROL KEYS
         420- 440 START LINE
         450   FLAG FOR LINE BREAK
         480   DRAW LINE
         490   UPDATE COUNTERS
         500- 570 PUT COORDINATE DATA INTO X,Y,W ARRAYS
         580   RESET COUNTERS FOR LINE BREAK
         590   SET SEGMENT COUNTER
         650- 680 TEMP LINE DRAW/WIPE

The cursor control section of SKETCH uses the joystick because this device gives much more convenient control over picture generation than does keyboard control.

The use of the X, Y, W and S arrays in SKETCH is essentially the same as for the programs we have already looked at. The new part of SKETCH is really the manipulation of the joystick and cursor for interactive data creation. Lines 180-330 of SKETCH handle cursor movement, and three main steps are involved. These are:

(1)   cursor plotting
(2)   cursor movement
(3)   cursor erasure

The cursor is plotted by drawing two straight lines, one horizontal, one vertical, which intersect at their midpoints. The length of these lines is set using the variable CS. If the plotted point is at coordinates x,y then the X line is drawn from x-CS,y to x+CS,y: the Y line is correspondingly drawn from x,y-CS to x,y+CS. Movement of the cursor occurs by using the values returned from the joystick to increment or decrement the x or y values. Re-plotting of the cursor can then occur around the new x,y point. For cursor erasure, a cursor is retraced around the original x,y point, but this time each pixel is cleared instead of being plotted. By using these three operations together, movement of the cursor around the screen may be smoothly controlled with the joystick.

3.5 How to use SKETCH

You will find SKETCH difficult to use at first. Drawing by 'remote control' is not an easy skill to master, but some quite impressive results can be obtained, as you see from the pictures reproduced below. Once you have acquired the skill of pressing the correct key or fire button at the right time you can produce useful data with the program. The pictures shown here were drawn using an additional trick. Each outline was traced on an A4 sheet of overhead transparency film (you can buy this at an art or business supplies shop). The film was then stuck onto the monitor screen using sticky tape. Using this method, it is then possible to sit back and trace the outline using the joystick and SKETCH. Try creating a map of some adjoining counties or US states with each state or county as a segment. Write a version of DRAW2D to enable you to recall segments in any order. Use your program to test your friends' knowledge of geography!

MAP OF ENGLAND AND WALES CREATED USING SKETCH PROGRAM 5/7/85

Figure 3.6 Output from SKETCH. A simple outline map of England and Wales

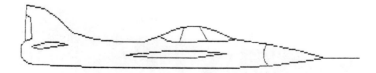

Figure 3.7 Output from SKETCH. A jet plane.

The use of SKETCH with transparency film in this way is an example of a makeshift digitizer, a device for directly transferring spatial data into the computer. Commercial digitizers can cost up to £20,000. Now you have one for the cost of a joystick!

If you have a CPC 6128 or CPC 664 you may like to add the following FILL routine to SKETCH. It works as follows. When you have drawn your picture, put the cursor in the centre of the area you wish to colour. Press the Z key. You then choose the colour by pressing the 1, 2 or 3 key. The area (make sure it is enclosed!) is then filled, and you are returned to the main program to draw more lines or to reselect further colours as you wish. The FILL routine does not affect the ability to save the picture, as the colouring process is transparent to the data structures holding points and lines.

```
217     K$=INKEY$:IF K$="Z"THEN GOSUB 4000:REM PAINT ROUTINE
4000 REM FILL ROUTINE FOR USE WITH SKETCH PROGRAM (ONLY ON CPC 664)
4010 REM USE WITH MODE 1 ONLY
4020 INK 2,3:INK 3,12
4025 MOVE X+2,Y+2
4030     K$=INKEY$
4040     IF K$=""THEN 4030
4050     IF K$="1"THEN FILL 1
4060     IF K$="2"THEN FILL 2
4070     IF K$="3"THEN FILL 3
4080 RETURN
```

SKETCH PROGRAM

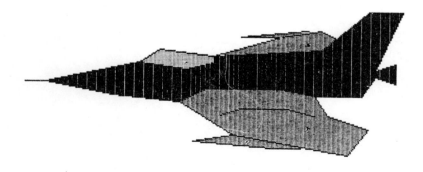

Figure 3.8 Output from SKETCH using the FILL amendment.

Chapter 4

Manipulating 2D Data

4.1 The coordinate system

In this chapter you will learn how to move two dimensional pictures and segments around on the screen. Before doing this, we will revise some of the elementary rules of two dimensional coordinate geometry. Although we have already looked at a number of simple programs which use X and Y coordinates, it will help if we look at the coordinate system in a little more detail.

In essence, we are dealing with a rectangular coordinate system. This consists of two scales called axes. One of the scales is horizontal, the other vertical. The point of intersection of the axes is called the origin. It is usual to designate the right side of the horizontal axis as the positive x axis, and the upward direction as the positive y axis. (It follows that the left side of the x axis and the downward direction on the y axis are therefore negative).

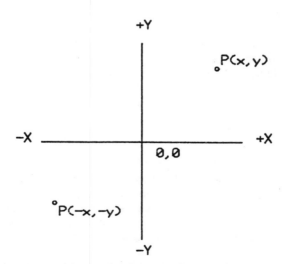

Figure 4.1 Labelling of axes in an X,Y coordinate system. Two points are shown, one positive and the other (with the same coordinates but different sign) negative.

The diagram above shows the layout of these axes. Using them, any point can be designated P(x,y) on any of the four sectors or quadrants around the origin depending on the sign of x and y. On most home computers (and all other computers I have worked with) the origin is at the bottom left hand corner of the screen. This means that all plotted coordinates must have positive values.

Now that we have seen how to represent points in a rectangular coordinate system, we can draw simple pictures on the screen using the commands **MOVE** and **DRAW**, together with the data held in a simple data structure. This is fine if all the data is within the bounds of the Amstrad screen coordinate area (X = 0 - 639, Y = 0 - 199), and if no spatial manipulations are to be done on the data. But what if we wish to move an object around on the screen, to change its size along one or both axes, or to rotate it around a specified axis?

The techniques for doing these operations are called *transformations* in graphics jargon, and the main ones are the 'holy trinity' of *rotation, scaling* and *translation*. Using combinations of these transformations, we can manipulate two dimensional pictures at will. Now although it is possible to perform all 2D transformations by a mixture of 'brute strength' arithmetic and basic trigonometry, we will use *matrix algebra* for all our transformations. Matrix algebra provides an extremely efficient system for manipulating coordinate data. The disadvantage is that in order to understand this form of manipulation you have to learn what matrices are, and how to handle them.

This is not to say that there is anything particularly complex about handling matrices, and details of how to go about doing it are given in Appendix 2. Reference to this appendix will be made throughout this section, but if mathematics truly does give you nightmares - don't worry! You do not need to understand the contents of Appendix 2 to be able to use the routines given here. In fact, it is quite possible for you to work through the whole book without knowing what matrices are: but don't be lazy - try Appendix 2 - like some new foreign dish, it may even appeal to your palate.

4.2 Rotation

As its name suggests, rotation involves turning the picture, or part of it, through an angle in space. We require an important piece of information before performing a rotation - the point around which the object is to be rotated. Although it is possible to mathematically compute a rotation around any given point in 2D space, by far the easiest point to rotate around is the origin. Using matrix algebra it is easy to set up a matrix A which, when evaluated, gives rotated x,y points around the origin for a given data set. Let us step through a simple two dimensional rotation program to see how it works.

The first step is to read in the data to the X,Y and W arrays that will be used for storage, and we saw how to do this in the last chapter. We will leave out the segment array for now in order to simplify the program. Next, we set up the correct matrix. For all 2D transformations our matrices will appear as arrays D I M'd 3 X 3. Here we will use the array A(3,3) to hold the matrix, and a rotation routine sets up the matrix. Finally, we mutiply the x,y data and the rotation matrix to transform the data. Our flow chart for this program might look something like the following:

Input x,y data
↓
Input rotation angle
↓
Set up rotation matrix
↓
Multiply each pair of x, y
points with the rotation matrix
↓
Plot picture using the
transformed points
↓
Loop to matrix
multiplication
step

The whole program appears below. If you type this in you will find that it draws an arrow which starts out along the Y axis and gradually moves down to the X axis.

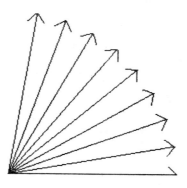

Figure 4.2 Output from ROTATE. Each arrow has been rotated + 10 degrees around the origin at 0,0.

You can clearly see that the origin is acting as the pivot point. The program calculates a sequence of 10 degree rotations, looping between lines 160 and 190. Note that the transformation matrix only has to be set up once: as each rotation is by 10 degrees it is only the matrix multiplications that need to be repeated. You will find these multiplications between lines 430 and 490. Note the use of the constant .17455 in line 160. This is ten degrees in radians, one degree being equal to .017455 radians (or approximately so - there are in fact 2 X pi radians in 360 degrees).

ROTATE program

```
10 REM ****PROGRAM ROTATE****
20 REM DEMONSTRATES 2D ROTATIONS USING MATRIX TRANSFORMATIONS
25 REM ROTATES ARROW AROUND ORIGIN 0,0
30 REM SET UP ARRAYS
40 DIM X(4),Y(4),XP(4),YP(4),LN(2,3),A(3,3),PO(3),P(3)
45 CLS
50 REM GET DATA TO DRAW SHAPE
60    READ NPTS
70    FOR I=1 TO NPTS
80    READ X(I),Y(I)
90    NEXT I
100   READ LI
110   FOR I=1 TO LI
120   READ LN(1,I),LN(2,I)
130   NEXT I
140 DATA 4,0,0,0,195,10,185,-10,185,3,1,2,2,3,2,4
150 REM NOW SET ROTATION ANGLE
160 AN=AN+0.174533
170   GOSUB 360:REM ROTATION ROUTINE
180   GOSUB 430:REM DRAW PICTURE
190 GOTO 160
200 END
220    A(1,1)=COS(AN):A(1,2)=SIN(AN):A(1,3)=0;
360 REM ROTATION ROUTINE
370   A(1,1)=COS(AN):A(1,2)=SIN(AN):A(1,3)=0
380   A(2,1)=-SIN(AN):A(2,2)=COS(AN):A(2,3)=0
390   A(3,1)=0:A(3,2)=0:A(3,3)=1
400 RETURN
430 REM SETUP PICTURE
440   FOR I=1 TO NPTS:P(1)=0:P(2)=0:P(3)=0
445   PO(1)=X(I):PO(2)=Y(I):PO(3)=1
450   FOR J=1 TO 3
455   FOR K=1 TO 3
460      P(J)=(A(J,K)*PO(K))+P(J)
470   NEXT K:NEXT J
480   XP(I)=P(1):YP(I)=P(2)
490   NEXT I
500 REM NOW DRAW THE PICTURE
```

```
510       FOR I=1 TO LI
520       MOVE XP(LN(1,I)),YP(LN(1,I))
530       DRAW XP(LN(2,I)),YP(LN(2,I))
540       NEXT I
550 RETURN
```

In ROTATE, you will see that we keep the original X Y data 'virgin', and the transformations are done on two new arrays called XP and YP. It is in fact quite usual to keep working or 'scratch' arrays to hold the coordinate data to be plotted on screen. In future programs you will find the arrays XP and YP used as a matter of course.

Although we have used matrix algebra to determine the rotated coordinates, it is possible, if the angle of rotation is not too large, to use a more elementary method, which is much faster, but it only works for increments of one or two degrees. The new coordinates for each point are then

$$x' = x - y \sin (\text{theta})$$

$$\text{and } y' = x' \sin (\text{theta}) + y$$

You can rewrite the arrow rotation program to draw, say, one degree rotations from 0 to 90 degrees to see the vast increase in speed that is produced. But see what a mess it makes if you set theta to something like ten degrees!

4.3 Translation

A translation is simply a reduction or increase of the X and/or Y coordinate values of the segment or whole picture. Translations are also performed by way of matrices, again using a 3 X 3 array to hold the matrix. We can easily amend the ROTATE program to accommodate translations. The translation matrix is set up using the following routine, which you can add to ROTATE. In the next few pages we will build up a general 2D transformation program, so we will call the program TRV.. from now on. This first version you could call TRV1

```
600   rem translation routine
610   a(1,1)=1:a(1,2)=0:a(1,3)=tx
620   a(2,1)=0:a(2,2)=1:a(2,3)=ty
630   a(3,1)=0:a(3,2)=0:a(3,3)=1
640   return
```

TX and TY are the changes in x and y coordinates of the points to be translated. These values must be set up in the program before the translation routine is called. If the TRV1 program is to translate the arrow along the X axis in increments of 10 screen units, for example, the following changes should also be made.

```
135  tx=10:ty=0:rem set translation step
170  gosub600:rem translation step
```

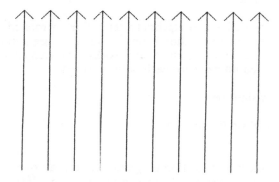

Figure 4.3 Output from TRV1. Each arrow has been translated + 10 pixels along the X axis.

Translation in general graphics programming is also a vital procedure. It allows us to move pictures or segments from and to the origin. We saw in the previous section that the easiest rotations to perform are those around the origin, and by using appropriate translations we can simulate rotation around any point in coordinate space. In order to do this, the following sequence is used.

(1) Translate the object to the origin
(2) Rotate the object
(3) Translate the object back to the original position

We can use the TRV1 program, with a few amendments, to perform this sequence you will no doubt appreciate by now that we are building TRV1 into a general program for performing two dimensional transformations). As both translation and rotation routines are already in TRV1, there is little more to add. Before looking at the use of translation and rotation together, the third type of transformation should be mentioned.

4.4 Scaling

Perhaps you have an object drawn in the centre of the screen and wish it to be expanded to occupy the whole area. Alternatively, you may wish to expand an object either horizontally or vertically. These operations are performed by increasing the relative distances between the coordinate points of the segment.

The following routine sets up a matrix to be used in scaling transformations. It follows the same pattern as the rotation and translation matrices, ie it is held in a 3 X 3 array A(3,3).

```
700   rem scale routine
710   a(1,1)=sx:a(1,2)=0:a(1,3)=0
720   a(2,1)=0:a(2,2)=sy:a(2,3)=0
730   a(3,1)=0:a(3,2)=0:a(3,3)=1
740   return
```

The variables sx and sy hold the values by which the x and y coordinates are to be respectively multiplied. If one of the axes is to remain unchanged, the variable should be set at 1, not 0. Reductions as well as increases in size can be used.

The following expansion of TRV1 (call this TRV2) demonstrates the use of all the transformations discussed so far in the same program. The program prompts for translation and scale values, and draws a small 'spaceship' with its minimum x and y coordinates at 10,10 (the bottom left corner). The sequence of transformations in the program is given between lines 240 - 290. Run the program to familiarise yourself with the effect that various parameter values have on the shape, size and position of the spaceship.

TRV2 program

```
10 REM ****PROGRAM TRANSFORMV2****
20 REM PROGRAM TO DO TRANSLATION, SCALE AND ROTATION ON SPACESHIP
30 DIM X(20),Y(20),LN(2,30),A(4,4),P(3),PO(3)
40 REM GET DATA TO DRAW SHAPE
```

```
50    READ NPTS
60    FOR I=1 TO NPTS:Z=3
70    READ X(I),Y(I)
80    NEXT I
90    READ LI
100   FOR I=1 TO LI
110   READ LN(1,I),LN(2,I)
120   NEXT I
130 REM DATA FOR SPACECHIP
140   DATA 11,10,10,10,30,20,40,20,60,25,70,30,60,30,40,40,30,40,10,30,20,20,20
150   DATA 11,1,2,2,3,3,4,4,5,5,6,6,7,7,8,8,9,9,10,10,11,11,1
160 REM INPUT TRANSFORMATION INFO
170   CLS
180   INPUT "TRANSLATION TX,TY?";TX,TY
190   INPUT "SCALING AMOUNTS SX,SY?";SX,SY
200   INPUT "ROTATION IN DEGREES?";AN
210 REM CHANGE ROTATION TO RADIANS
220   AN=AN*0.017455
230 REM NOW DO THE TRANSFORMATIONS
240   T1=-X(1):T2=-Y(1):REM TRANSLATE TO ORIGIN
250 GOSUB 360:REM TRANSLATION ROUTINE
260 GOSUB 510:REM DRAW PICTURE
270 GOSUB 410:REM SCALE ROUTINE
280 GOSUB 510:REM DRAW PICTURE
290 GOSUB 460:REM ROTATION ROUTINE
300 GOSUB 510:REM DRAW PICTURE
310 T1=TX:T2=TY
320 GOSUB 360:REM TRANSLATION ROUTINE
330 GOSUB 510:REM DRAW PICTURE
340 END
360 REM TRANSLATION ROUTINE
365   A(1,1)=1:A(1,2)=0:A(1,3)=T1
370   A(2,1)=0:A(2,2)=1:A(2,3)=T2
375   A(3,1)=0:A(3,2)=0:A(3,3)=1
380 RETURN
410 REM SCALE ROUTINE
420   A(1,1)=SX:A(1,2)=0:A(1,3)=0
425   A(2,1)=0 :A(2,2)=SY:A(2,3)=0
430   A(3,1)=0 :A(3,2)=0:A(3,3)=1
440 RETURN
460 REM ROTATION ROUTINE
465   A(1,1)=COS(AN):A(1,2)=SIN(AN):A(1,3)=0
470   A(2,1)=-SIN(AN):A(2,2)=COS(AN):A(2,3)=0
475   A(3,1)=0:A(3,2)=0:A(3,3)=1
480 RETURN
510 REM PROCESS POINTS FOR PICTURE
520   FOR I=1 TO NPTS
525      P(1)=0:P(2)=0:P(3)=0
530      P0(1)=X(I):P0(2)=Y(I):P0(3)=1
540   FOR J=1 TO 3
545   FOR K=1 TO 3
550      P(J)=(A(J,K)*P0(K))+P(J)
555   NEXT K
560   NEXT J
```

```
565        X(I)=P(1)
570        Y(I)=P(2)
575    NEXT I
580 REM NOW DRAW THE PICTURE
600    FOR I=1 TO LI
610        MOVE X(LN(1,I)),Y(LN(1,I))
620        DRAW X(LN(2,I)),Y(LN(2,I))
630    NEXT I
640 FOR I=1 TO 1000:NEXT I
650 RETURN
```

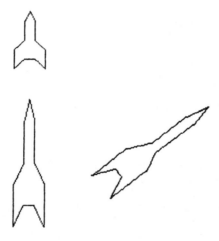

Figure 4.4 Output from TRV2. Spaceship (1) has been scaled up, rotated (2) and finally translated to a new location (3).

4.5 Sequences of transformations

The simplest sequences of transformations have already been covered: translation to the origin, rotation, translation back to the final position. We used a rather laborious method for doing the transformation sequence in TRV2, admittedly, for the purpose of demonstration. In fact, the intermediate stage of translation back to the origin and out again can be accomplished without intermediate calculation of coordinate positions. As you will see if you read Appendix 2, the secret is to multiply the series of 3 X 3 matrices for rotation, scaling and translation together as soon as they have been set up. We can use a single routine to take care of this within the transformation program. Matrix multiplication is not complicated, but care has to be taken to do the multiplications in the correct order: although A X B = B X A in school algebra, matrix multiplication of A X B does not necessarily give the same product as B X A. The rules for matrix multiplication will be found in Appendix 2. Here is the routine for multiplying two 3 X 3 matrices. Note that this is rather different from the matrix multiplications which you have already met in the TRV2 program. This is because the multiplications in this case were performed between the transformation array and the coordinate data only. Again, this will be made clearer in Appendix 2 if you want to know the nuts and bolts of what is going on.

```
3000 rem routine matrixmultiplier
3010 rem the two matrices must be in arrays
     dimensioned a(3,3) and b(3,3)
3020 for i=1 to 3
3030 for j=1 to 3:ab=0
3040 for k=1 to 3
3050 ab=ab+a(i,k)"b(k,j)
3060 nextk:c(i,j)=ab:nextj:nexti
3070 return
```

Now let us put this routine into our expanded TRV2 program. Unfortunately, it is not possible to merely slot the routine into TRV2, because several multiplications have to be done, and as you will see from the new version below, some complexities are encountered. The end result is to produce a 'super' matrix product which is used for the final coordinate calculations. This final version of the transformation program (TRV3) also contains a file read section to allow input of data from a file created with SKETCH or FILE2D.

TRV3 program

```
10 REM ****PROGRAM TRANSFORMV3****
20 REM DOES 2D TRANSFORMATIONS ON,DATA IN FILE CREATED USING SKETCH OR FILE2D
30 CLS
40 INPUT"FILENAME?";H$
45 OPENIN H$
50 INPUT£9,NPTS
55 DIM A(3,3),B(3,3),C(3,3)
60 DIM X(NPTS),Y(NPTS),XP(NPTS),YP(NPTS)
65 XL=640:XH=0:YL=400:YH=0
```

```
70    FOR I=1 TO NPTS
75      INPUT£9,X(I),Y(I)
80      REM SORT FOR MAX AND MIN VALS
85      IF X(I)<XL THEN XL=X(I)
90      IF X(I)>XH THEN XH=X(I)
95      IF Y(I)<YL THEN YL=Y(I)
100     IF Y(I)>YH THEN YH=Y(I)
110   NEXT I
120     INPUT£9,LI
125 DIM LN(2,LI)
130   FOR I=1 TO LI
135     INPUT£9,LN(1,I),LN(2,I)
140   NEXT I
150 CLOSEIN
160 REM INPUT TRANSFORMATION INFO
165   INPUT"TRANSLATION TX,TY";TX,TY
170   INPUT"SCALING AMOUNTS";SX,SY
180   INPUT"ROTATION IN DEGREES";AN
185   AN=AN*0.017455:REM RADIANS
190 REM NOW PUT COORDINATE DATA INTO TEMPORARY ARRAYS
192   FOR I=1 TO NPTS
194     XP(I)=X(I)
196     YP(I)=Y(I)
198   NEXT I
200 GOSUB 2500:REM DRAW ORIGINAL PICTURE
210 REM NOW DO THE TRANSFORMATIONS
220 T1=-((XH+XL)/2):T2=-((YH+YL)/2):REM TRANSLATE CENTRE POINT TO ORIGIN
230 REM SETUP MATRICES AND DO MULTIPLICATIONS
275 GOSUB 1400:REM ROTATION (MATRIX A)
280 GOSUB 1100:REM TRANSLATION (MATRIX B) TO ORIGIN
300 GOSUB 1600:REM FIRST MULTIPLICATION (MATRIX C)
310 GOSUB 1500:REM ROTATION (MATRIX B)
315 GOSUB 1300:REM SCALING (MATRIX B)
320 GOSUB 1700:REM SECOND MULTIPLICATION (MATRIX A)
330 T1=-T1+TX:T2=-T2+TY:REM SET TRANSLATION VALUES
340 GOSUB 1100:REM TRANSLATION (MATRIX B)
350 GOSUB 1600:REM THIRD MULTIPLICATION (MATRIX C)
360 GOSUB 2000:REM NOW WORK OUT COORDINATES
370 GOSUB 2500:REM DRAW PICTURE
380 INPUT X:IF X=1 THEN CLS:GOTO 160
400 END
1000 REM TRANSLATION ROUTINE
1010   A(1,1)=1:A(1,2)=0:A(1,3)=T1
1020   A(2,1)=0:A(2,2)=1:A(2,3)=T2
1030   A(3,1)=0:A(3,2)=0:A(3,3)=1
1040 RETURN
1100 REM TRANSLATION ROUTINE
1110   B(1,1)=1:B(1,2)=0:B(1,3)=T1
1120   B(2,1)=0:B(2,2)=1:B(2,3)=T2
1130   B(3,1)=0:B(3,2)=0:B(3,3)=1
1140 RETURN
1250 REM SCALE ROUTINE
1260   A(1,1)=SX:A(1,2)=0:A(1,3)=0
1270   A(2,1)=0 :A(2,2)=SY:A(2,3)=0
```

```
1280    A(3,1)=0 :A(3,2)=0:A(3,3)=1
1290 RETURN
1300 REM SCALE ROUTINE
1310    B(1,1)=SX:B(1,2)=0:B(1,3)=0
1320    B(2,1)=0 :B(2,2)=SY:B(2,3)=0
1330    B(3,1)=0 :B(3,2)=0:B(3,3)=1
1340 RETURN
1400 REM ROTATION ROUTINE
1410    A(1,1)=COS(AN):A(1,2)=SIN(AN):A(1,3)=0
1420    A(2,1)=-SIN(AN):A(2,2)=COS(AN):A(2,3)=0
1430    A(3,1)=0:A(3,2)=0:A(3,3)=1
1440    RETURN
1500 REM ROTATION ROUTINE
1510    B(1,1)=COS(AN):B(1,2)=SIN(AN):B(1,3)=0
1520    B(2,1)=-SIN(AN):B(2,2)=COS(AN):B(2,3)=0
1530    B(3,1)=0:B(3,2)=0:B(3,3)=1
1540    RETURN
1600 REM MATRIX MULTIPLIER (RESULT IN C)
1610    FOR I=1 TO 3
1620    FOR J=1 TO 3:AB=0
1630    FOR K=1 TO 3
1640      AB=AB+A(I,K)*B(K,J)
1650    NEXT K
1660      C(I,J)=AB
1670    NEXT J
1680    NEXT I
1690 RETURN
1700 REM MATRIX MULTIPLIER (RESULT IN A)
1710    FOR I=1 TO 3
1720    FOR J=1 TO 3:AB=0
1730    FOR K=1 TO 3
1740      AB=AB+B(I,K)*C(K,J)
1750    NEXT K
1760      A(I,J)=AB
1770    NEXT J
1780    NEXT I
1790 RETURN
2000 REM PROCESS POINTS FOR PICTURE
2010    FOR I=1 TO NPTS
2020      P(1)=0:P(2)=0:P(3)=0
2030        PO(1)=XP(I):PO(2)=YP(I):PO(3)=1
2040    FOR J=1 TO 3
2050    FOR K=1 TO 3
2060        P(J)=(C(J,K)*PO(K))+P(J)
2070    NEXT K
2080    NEXT J
2090      XP(I)=P(1)
2100      YP(I)=P(2)
2110    NEXT I
2500 REM NOW DRAW THE PICTURE
2510    FOR I=1 TO LI
2520      MOVE XP(LN(1,I)),YP(LN(1,I))
2530        DRAW XP(LN(2,I)),YP(LN(2,I))
2540    NEXT I
```

80

```
2550 FOR I=1 TO 1000:NEXT I
2560 RETURN
```

If you look at lines 1000-1540 of TRV3, you can see that the matrices are set up in exactly the same way as was used in TRV2, but the actual routines for each transformation are duplicated for each type of transformation. This is necessary because the multiplications require the matrices to be in either arrays A and B, or B and C. The C matrix is in fact the product resulting from the multiplication of matrices A and B, while the product of B and C is put into array A.

The matrix multiplication that gives the coordinates for plotting (lines 2000-2110) uses the C array as the final transformation matrix. You must bear this in mind when amending TRV3.

You should try variations in the data set and transformation sequences to make sure that you have grasped how to handle these matrix manipulations. By manipulating some complex outlines with SKETCH, you will be able to gauge the speed at which the various transformations work in BASIC.

4.6 Windows on the world

We now need to introduce two terms which you will come across in articles and books on computer graphics. These terms are *window* and *viewport*. The diagram below shows how they are related. If you think of a two dimensional scene as being the two dimensional 'world' which we wish to display, then the window is the part of that world to be displayed on the screen.

For many simpler applications, there may be a one-to-one relationship between window and world - the shapes that we have used for our examples so far come into this category. But other pictures require different parts of the world to be displayed. We therefore need to define a window which can be positioned at any point over the 2D world. Consider for example a map or circuit diagram. The total amount of information in pictures of these types will be far greater than that which could be displayed on the screen at the same time. Use of the windowing technique allows any subpart of a picture to be displayed on its own. You may wish to 'scroll' over a map for example, and providing the window and scrolling facility are coupled to a suitable data set, this will be possible.

The viewport is simply the part of the screen on which the window is displayed. Viewports are useful if different parts of the screen are to be used to display different things: an example would be if part of the screen is to be used for graphics and part for text. The ability to separate text and graphics in this way

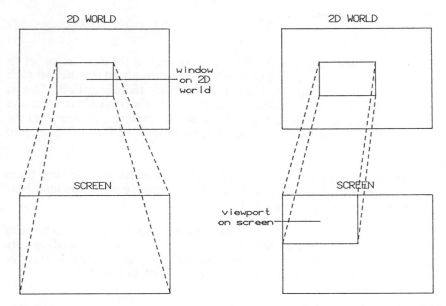

Figure 4.5 The relationship between the 2D world, windows and viewports. A mapping of 1:1 between 2D world and screen would give a window the size of the 2D world and a viewport the size of the screen.

is inherent in the Amstrad computers via the **WINDOW** command. You should note that WINDOW only allows text streams to be manipulated separately. Graphics commands are not associated with streams and cannot be 'windowed' via Amstrad BASIC. If window and viewport techniques are used together, the effects of zooming and panning can be simulated. Program ZOOM below shows how these operations can be done using BASIC. Note that the following statements hold true.

(1)   If you decrease the window size but keep the viewport constant you produce 'zooming in'.
(2)   If you increase the window size but keep the viewport constant you produce 'zooming out'.
(3)   If you move the window you produce 'panning'.

The window size can be changed dynamically during execution of ZOOM by pressing the S key (this makes the window smaller) and the L key (making the window larger). The joystick is used to move over the surface of the displayed picture, and when the window is the correct size and is positioned over the correct part of the picture, pressing the fire button followed by the space bar performs the zoom operation. To return to the original picture, the fire button is again pressed, followed by key N.

You can use ZOOM to look at a 2D space that is much larger than the Amstrad's 640 X 400 coordinate space, and conversely, you can expand a smaller picture to fill the whole screen. Here is an example of the output from ZOOM

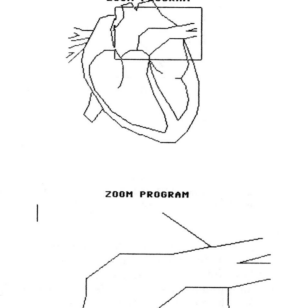

Figure 4.6 Output from ZOOM. A human heart. Note the position of the cursor window defining the 'zoomed' area in the lower picture.

Apart from translation and scaling (operations at which you are, by now, expert!) ZOOM uses the concept of *clipping*. Clipping means that lines passing out of the chosen window are 'cut' at the window's edge, like this

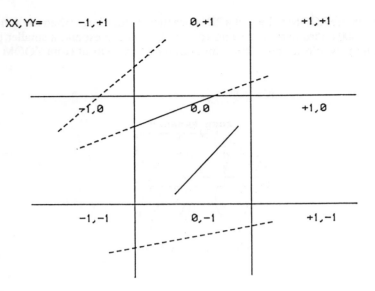

Figure 4.7 The clipping operation. The screen is divided into nine rectangles, with the visible space in the centre rectangle. Note that the values of XX and YY are set to 1 if they are > the visible space, 0 if they are inside the visible space, and -1 if they are < the visible space.

The algorithm used to do this clipping is a standard one devised some years ago by US graphics pioneer Ivan Sutherland, and consists of 'moving' all the ends of lines passing out of the window to the point on the window's edge on the line. The clipping algorithm is found between lines 160-1540 of ZOOM, and works as follows. If you look at the previous diagram, you'll see that the whole area is divided up into nine rectangles, with the positions of the vertical and horizontal lines being set by the position, shape and size of the window to be clipped to.

Every point on the screen will be in one of the rectangles, and we use this information as the basis for the algorithm. As you can see from the diagram, the rectangles are identified by the values of two variables, XX and YY. If XX and YY are 0 for both points on a line, we know that the whole line is visible within the window. If XX is -1 or +1 then no matter what the value of YY, the line will totally fall outside the window. If YY is -1 or +1 the line will also be outside the window. In the other cases there is a possibility (not a certainty) that part of the line will be inside the window, and one or perhaps both points on the ends of the line will be outside the window.

In these cases, the position of the point outside the window will be moved onto the edge of the window (for example c' in the previous diagram).

The algorithm uses two routines: TYPE returns the XX and YY values to identify the rectangle for each point in the picture. CLIP uses this information to move the points outside the window to the window edge as required.

ZOOM program

```
5 REM ****PROGRAM ZOOM****
10 REM TAKES PICTURE IN FILE2D FORMAT AND EXPANDS SECTION BOUNDED BY A WINDOW
20 REM SET I,J,K,L,R VARIABLES TO INTEGER
30 DEFINT I,J,K,L,R
40 CLS:MODE 2
45 GOSUB 1500:REM TITLES
50 LOCATE 1,1:INPUT "FILENAME?";H$
60 OPENIN H$
70      INPUT£9,NPTS
80      DIM X(NPTS),Y(NPTS)
90      FOR I=1 TO NPTS
100         INPUT£9,X(I),Y(I)
110     NEXT I
120     INPUT£9,LI
130     DIM LN(2,LI)
140     FOR I=1 TO LI
150         INPUT£9,LN(1,I),LN(2,I)
160     NEXT I
170 CLOSEIN
180 REM INPUT CLIPPING INFORMATION
190     XW=640:YW=400
200     K$="N"
210     XC=320:YC=200:REM SET CENTRE POINT
220     ZX=1:ZY=1
230     WX=40:WY=INT(40*0.625):X=320:Y=200:WW=5
240     DX=XW/2:DY=YW/2
250 REM CLIPPING SECTION
260         XM=(640*ZX)/XW
270         YM=(400*ZY)/YW
280     REM DO TITLE
300         FOR I=1 TO LI
310             X1=X(LN(1,I))-XC
320             Y1=Y(LN(1,I))-YC
330             X2=X(LN(2,I))-XC
340             Y2=Y(LN(2,I))-YC
350         IF K$="N" THEN XM=1:GOTO 660
360         XT=X1:YT=Y1:GOSUB 860:REM CLIP MODE
370         I1=R1:I2=R2
380         XT=X2:YT=Y2:GOSUB 860:REM CLIP MODE
390         I3=R1:I4=R2
400         REM ARE ALL POINTS OUT OF THE WINDOW?
410         IF(I1*I3=1) OR (I2*I4=1) THEN 710
420         IF I1=0 THEN 490
```

85

```
430    REM MOVE POINT 1'S COORDINATE TO WINDOW EDGE
440     XX=DX*I1
450     Y1=Y1+(Y2-Y1)*(XX-X1)/(X2-X1)
460     X1=XX
470     XT=X1:YT=Y1:GOSUB 860:REM CLIP MODE
480     I1=R1:I2=R2
490     IF I2=0 THEN 540
500    REM MOVE POINT 1'S Y COORDINATE TO WINDOW EDGE
510     YY=DY*I2
520     X1=X1+(X2-X1)*(YY-Y1)/(Y2-Y1)
530     Y1=YY
540     IF I3=0 THEN 590
550    REM MOVE POINT 2'S X COORDINATE TO WINDOW EDGE
560     XX=DX*I3
570     Y2=Y1+(Y2-Y1)*(XX-X1)/(X2-X1)
580     X2=XX
590     XT=X2:YT=Y2:GOSUB 860:REM CLIP MODE
600     I3=R1:I4=R2
610     IF I4=0 THEN 660
620    REM MOVE POINT 2'S Y COORDINATE TO WINDOW EDGE
630     YY=DY*I4
640     X2=X1+(X2-X1)*(YY-Y1)/(Y2-Y1)
650     Y2=YY
660     REM YOU ARE NOW READY TO PLOT
670         X1=(X1*XM)+320:X2=(X2*XM)+320
680         Y1=(Y1*YM)+200:Y2=(Y2*YM)+200
690             MOVE X1,Y1
700             DRAW X2,Y2
710     NEXT I
720 REM NOW HANDLE THE WINDOW OUTLINE DISPLAY
730     GOSUB 960:REM WINDOW PLOT
740     GOSUB 1030:REM WINDOW MOVE
750     GOSUB 1160:REM TOGGLE WINDOW SIZE
760 IF JOY(0)<>16 THEN 720
765 CLS:GOSUB 1500
770     XW=X2-X1:YW=Y2-Y1:XC=X:YC=Y'
775 GOTO 240
850 END
860 REM SUBROUTINE CLIP MODE
870     R1=0:R2=0
880         IF ABS(XT)>DX THEN R1=1:IF XT<0 THEN R1=-1
890         IF ABS(YT)>DY THEN R2=1:IF YT<0 THEN R2=-1
900 RETURN
950 REM WINDOW PLOT ROUTINE
960     X1=X-WX:Y1=Y-WY:X2=X+WX:Y2=Y+WY
970         MOVE X1,Y1
980         DRAW X2,Y1,1,1
990         DRAW X2,Y2,1,1
1000        DRAW X1,Y2,1,1
1010        DRAW X1,Y1,1,1
1020 RETURN
1030 REM WINDOW MOVE ROUTINE
1040    Y3=Y:X3=X
1050        IF JOY(0)=4 THEN X=X-WW:GOTO 1090
```

```
1060      IF JOY(0)=8 THEN X=X+WW:GOTO 1090
1070      IF JOY(0)=1 THEN Y=Y+WW:GOTO 1090
1080     IF JOY(0)=2 THEN Y=Y-WW:GOTO 1090
1090         MOVE X1,Y1
1100         DRAW X2,Y1,1,1
1110         DRAW X2,Y2,1,1
1120         DRAW X1,Y2,1,1
1130         DRAW X1,Y1,1,1
1140 RETURN
1150 REM TOGGLE WINDOW SIZE ROUTINE
1160 K$=INKEY$:IF K$="S"THEN WX=WX-2:WY=WY-1.25
1170 IF K$="L"THEN WX=WX+2:WY=WY+1.25
1172 IF K$="N" THEN CLS:GOSUB 1500:GOTO 180
1180         MOVE X1,Y1
1190         DRAW X2,Y1,1,1
1200         DRAW X2,Y2,1,1
1210         DRAW X1,Y2,1,1
1220         DRAW X1,Y1,1,1
1230         DRAW X2,Y1,1,1
1240         DRAW X2,Y2,1,1
1250         DRAW X1,Y2,1,1
1260         DRAW X1,Y1,1,1
1270 RETURN
1500 REM TITLES
1510 LOCATE 34,1:PRINT"ZOOM PROGRAM"
1520 LOCATE 1,25:PRINT"  L=ENLARGE WINDOW   S=SHRINK WINDOW   FIRE=ZOOM   N=NORMAL
     SIZE PICTURE
1530 MOVE 0,30
1540 DRAW 640,30
1550 RETURN
```

The main sections of ZOOM are as follows.

The data for ZOOM is read in from any 2D data file that uses the standard format that we have employed in SKETCH and FILE2D. This makes it a useful way of enlarging parts of a complex data set. If the original data has been created on screen using SKETCH however, there is a limit to the value of ZOOM. The ZOOM effect is much more dramatic if you are able to 'walk around' a picture that is made up of data originally drawn at many times the screen size. There are several ways of producing data larger than the screen, either using FILE2D, or by modifying SKETCH. The following version of SKETCH (called QUADRANT) allows a picture 4X screen size to be created using the SKETCH technique. As its name suggests, QUADRANT defines successive segments as quadrants of the final picture. The top left quadrant is segment one, top right is segment two, bottom left is segment three and bottom right is segment four. The final picture is therefore built up as shown in Figure 4.8

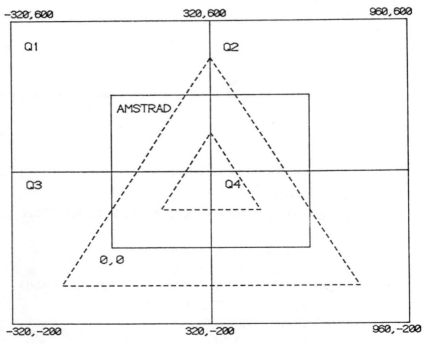

Figure 4.8 The four quadrants defined by QUADRANT. Note that the window extends from -320,200 to 960,600. The following transformation scales points drawn in this area into the normal Amstrad screen coordinate system.

$$XPLOT = (320 + X)/2$$
$$YPLOT = (200 + Y)/2$$

The dotted triangles show the effect of scaling.

To change SKETCH to QUADRANT, you need to make the following changes:

QUADRANT program

```
1 REM ****QUADRANT ADDITIONS FOR SKETCH****
2 REM TO ADD THESE LINES LOAD SKETCH FIRST AND THEN MERGE "QUADRANT"
3 QU=1:REM SET QUADRANT COUNTER
135 GOSUB 2700:REM CHANGE TEXT DISPLAY FOR QUADRANT
750 REM OVERWRITE THIS LINE
755  GOSUB 2500 :REM ADJUST SEGMENT COORDINATES
757 REM OVERWRITE THIS LINE
770 IF QU=5 THEN 800
2100 REM ROUTINE BOUNDARY_ADJUST
2110    IF X<0 THEN X=0
2120    IF X>640 THEN X=640
2130    IF Y<0 THEN Y=0
2140    IF Y>400 THEN Y=400
2150    IF XI<0 THEN XI=0
2160    IF XI>640 THEN XI=640
2170    IF YI<0 THEN YI=0
2180    IF YI>400 THEN YI=400
2190 RETURN
2500 REM QUADRANT COORDINATE ADJUST ROUTINE
2510 I1=LN(1,S(1,QU)):I2=LN(2,S(2,QU))
2520 FOR I=I1 TO I2
2530    IF QU=1 THEN XP(I)=XP(I)-320:YP(I)=YP(I)+200:GOTO 2600
2540    IF QU=2 THEN XP(I)=XP(I)+320:YP(I)=YP(I)+200:GOTO 2600
2550    IF QU=3 THEN XP(I)=XP(I)-320:YP(I)=YP(I)-200:GOTO 2600
2560    IF QU=4 THEN XP(I)=XP(I)+320:YP(I)=YP(I)-200:GOTO 2600
2600 NEXT I
2610 QU=QU+1
2620 IF QU=5 THEN GOTO 800
2630 GOSUB 2700
2640 RETURN
2700 REM TEXT FOR QUADRANT NUMBER
2702 CLS
2705 LOCATE 12,1:PRINT "QUADRANT PROGRAM"
2710    LOCATE 1,2
2720    PRINT "QUADRANT NO = ";QU
2730    LOCATE 1,23
2740    PRINT "PRESS E TO END QUADRANT"
2800 REM DIRECTION FINDER ROUTINE
2805  IF QU=1 THEN X9=47:Y9=298
2810  IF QU=2 THEN X9=563:Y9=298
2815  IF QU=3 THEN X9=47:Y9=99
2820 IF QU=4 THEN X9=563:Y9=99
2825  REM NOW DRAW THE FOUR SQUARES
2830    FOR I=1 TO 4
2835    IF I=2 THEN X9=X9+25
2840    IF I=3 THEN Y9=Y9+25
```

```
2845    IF I=4 THEN X9=X9-25
2850    MOVE X9,Y9:REM MOVE TO RELATIVE START POSITION FOR KEY
2855    DRAWR 20,0
2860    DRAWR 0,-20
2865    DRAWR -20,0
2870    DRAWR 0,20
2875 NEXT I
2880    IF QU=1 THEN LOCATE 4,6:PRINT"1"
2885    IF QU=2 THEN LOCATE 38,6:PRINT"2"
2890    IF QU=3 THEN LOCATE 4,20:PRINT"3"
2895    IF QU=4 THEN LOCATE 38,20:PRINT"4"
2900 REM GRID DRAWING ROUTINE
2905 REM NOTE MASK COMMAND FOR DOTTED LINES ONLY IN CPC664 BASIC
2910 FOR I=0 TO 640 STEP 40
2920 MOVE I,0
2930 MASK 36:DRAW I,400
2950 NEXT I
2955 FOR I=0 TO 400 STEP 40
2960 MOVE 0,I
2965 MASK 36:DRAW 640,I
2970 NEXT I
2975 MASK 255
2980 RETURN
```

The data produced by QUADRANT is in the range -320,-200 to 960,600. This gives a 'resolution' of 1280 X 800 pixels, although of course this cannot be directly seen on the Amstrad screen. An amended version of ZOOM (called ZOOMQUAD) is used to handle this data, and the necessary changes to ZOOM are given below. Operationally, ZOOMQUAD is identical to ZOOM, so the joystick and control keys are used in the same way in both versions.

The amendments to ZOOM to obtain ZOOMQUAD are rather less severe than those needed to produce QUADRANT. Here they are:

```
10 REM ****ZOOMQUAD VERSION OF ZOOM****
105 X(I)=(X(I)+320)/2:Y(I)=(Y(I)+200)/2
```

QUADRANT was used to create the map of the USA shown in the following screen dumps from ZOOMQUAD.

L=ENLARGE WINDOW   S=SHRINK WINDOW   FIRE=ZOOM   N=NORMAL SIZE PICTURE

Figure 4.9 Output from ZOOMQUAD: a map of the USA defined using QUADRANT on four separate segments (ie NW, NE, SW, SE): note the 'window' cursor.

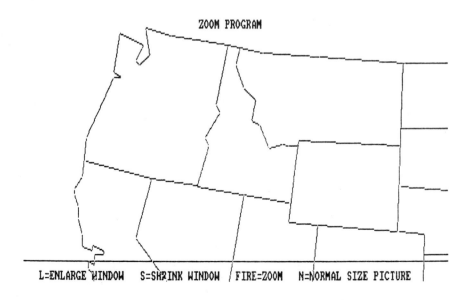

Figure 4.10 A detail of an area from the same map.

In this chapter we've seen a lot of fundamental 2D graphics techniques. The time has now come to put them all together to produce a 'useful' program. Now there are strict limits to what you can do in BASIC, because the poor old BASIC interpreter just cannot work quickly enough to do lengthy series of matrix multiplications in real time. This limitation is pretty well absolute if you wish to program a fast moving game or perhaps a flight simulator. We have already seen that it is possible to use a 'shortcut' method to carry out 2D rotations, and we will discuss other ways of overcoming speed limitations in the chapters on three dimensional graphics. But don't lose heart completely. Whatever your motives for learning graphics techniques, you won't get very far unless you have the armoury of techniques like those in this chapter at your disposal. Even if you are going to program in machine code, the algorithms will essentially be the same!

But even if you are now tempted to heave a sigh because you want to stick to BASIC, all is still not lost. Many applications are not shoot-em-up type games and do not need animation effects. The whole of Chapter 6 will be devoted to a description of one such application: a computer-aided-design program. This program demonstrates what I hope is a non-trivial use of all the routines set out in the present chapter.

Chapter 5
Business Graphics

5.1 The importance of presentation

Computer graphics are extensively used in the business area as aids to marketing studies, financial analysis and planning. Graphics are used to create graphs and charts to show data such as sales trends, comparative sales, cash flow and budget fluctuations. Information can be understood in graphical form more quickly than a corresponding page of figures, and the impact of a picture is much greater than more abstract data.

There are three main types of business graphics techniques. The first of these is the graph, and we saw an example of a simple graph program in Chapter 1. Graphs are most useful for displaying accurate data, if for example a large number of data points are to be illustrated. A variation on the graph theme is shown by the histogram, or bar chart. A bar chart shows graph data in a 'stepped' form and provides more scope for attractive layout. The third business graphics technique is use of a pie chart, where relative proportions of totals (ie 'slices of the pie') are illustrated by a sectored circle.

Business graphics packages available on the commercial market often display visually appealing and complex pictures by use of sophisticated software. It may even be possible to display several different treatments of the same data (for example histogram and graph) on screen at the same time. Fortunately for the home computer owner, the techniques of business graphics are really very simple. The complexity of graphics packages is usually due to the large amount of error trapping necessary to make them 'user friendly'. The Amstrad owner has an additional piece of good fortune. The Amstrad screen has an 80 column mode that allows much more professional looking business graphics to be produced that can be developed on most other home computers. So just what can be done on an Amstrad machine?

5.2 A slice of the pie

We have already looked at an algorithm for circle generation in the CIRCLE program (Chapter 1), and circle generation is the major constituent of a pie chart program. The important thing to remember about pie chart data is that is must be expressed in terms of proportions of the whole. You can therefore use a pie chart to display the relative sales of Widgets in different sales areas, but you would not use this method to plot sales over a twelve month period. The raw data for a pie chart might therefore look as follows.

Area	Widget Sales
London	10,100
South-East	17,300
Midlands	9,000
North	2,000
Scotland	1,600
	40,000 total

This data tells us a number of things. First, the pie will have five sectors (one for each area). Next, the regional sales will all be represented in the pie chart as a proportion of the total sales figure: it is easiest to think of this in percentage terms, so the percentage of sales in the London region is therefore

$$\frac{10,100}{40,000} \quad X \quad \frac{100}{1}$$

or 25.25 percent.

The first task of a pie chart program is to input the data, to total it, and to work out the proportions of each item in the total. But how do the radial sectors on the pie correspond to raw percentages? A pie chart consists of a number of lines radiating from a centre point with two adjacent lines indicating the proportion of a particular item. The angle between each pair of lines is therefore crucial. Instead of 100 percentage points to sum all the data, we have the 360 degree arc of a full circle. If we take the percentage of any item, the angle between the lines representing its boundaries on a pie chart will be

$$\frac{\text{item percentage}}{100} \quad X \quad 360 \text{ degrees}$$

The next task of the pie chart program is therefore to calculate the angular equivalents of the percentage data. The only other fundamental technique you need to write your own pie chart program is a method for calculating the radial lines. This uses the identical equations to those used to generate the circumference of a circle. Recall from the CIRCLE program that any point on the circumference of a circle has its X and Y coordinates defined by the equations

$$X = XC + (RADIUS * COS(ANGLE))$$

$$Y = YC + (RADIUS * SIN(ANGLE))$$

Where XC,YC are the coordinates of the circle centre.

So the radial lines defining the first segment of the pie, assuming the angle is known, will be defined by the lines

```
MOVE XC,YC
DRAW X,Y where ANGLE = 0
MOVE XC,YC
DRAW X1,Y1 where ANGLE = proportion for first segment
```

Now monochrome pies are very boring. This raises a problem on the CPC664 and CPC464, because 80 column mode only allows two colours on screen at any one time. You therefore have a trade-off between small (and hence neat) text but no colour, or chunky text and four colours in MODE 1. If you really want a rainbow coloured pie chart, use MODE 0. The text in MODE 0 is unfortunately so large that you will have to restrict yourself to one or at most two letter labels. The choice is yours. The following program PIE uses MODE 1, but can easily be amended for MODEs 0 or 2

PIE program

```
10 REM **** PROGRAM PIE ****
20 REM DRAWS A LABELLED PIE CHART 'USING FOUR COLOURS IN MODE 1
30 REM INPUT DATA
40 CLS:INK 0,13:INK 1,0:INK 2,3:INK 3,7
50 MODE 1
60 PRINT"    WELCOME TO THE PIE CHART PROGRAM"
65 INPUT"MAIN TITLE?";M$
66 P1=LEN(M$):P1=20-(P1/2)
70 INPUT"HOW MANY SEGMENTS FOR DISPLAY?";NUMBER
72 DIM S(NUMBER),H$(NUMBER),POINT(NUMBER),CUM(NUMBER)
73 TOTAL=0:CANGLE=0
75 FOR I=1 TO NUMBER
80 INPUT"INPUT THIS SEGMENT TITLE";H$(I)
85 INPUT"INPUT SEGMENT VALUE";S(I)
87 TOTAL=TOTAL+S(I)
90 NEXT I
100    FOR I=1 TO NUMBER:REM SET ANGLES FOR EACH SEGMENT
110    CANGLE=CANGLE+((S(I)/TOTAL)*(2*PI))
120    POINT(I)=CANGLE-(((S(I)/2)/TOTAL)*(2*PI))
122    CUM(I)=CANGLE
130    NEXT I
```

```
135 CLS
200 LOCATE P1,1:PRINT M$
205 TAG
220 REM SET CIRCLE SIZE
230 RADIUS=150
240 XC=320:YC=200
250     A=(2*PI)/100
260     ANGLE=0
270 X2=XC+RADIUS:Y2=YC
280   FOR I=1 TO 100
290     ANGLE=ANGLE+A
300     X1=X2:Y1=Y2
310     X2=XC+RADIUS*COS(ANGLE)
320     Y2=YC+RADIUS*SIN(ANGLE)
330     MOVE X1,Y1
340     DRAW X2,Y2
350 NEXT I
400 REM NOW PLOT SEGMENTS
405 N=-1
410 FOR I=1 TO NUMBER
415     N=N+1:IF N=4 THEN N=0
420     MOVE XC,YC
430     X1=XC+RADIUS*COS(CUM(I))
440     Y1=YC+RADIUS*SIN(CUM(I))
450     DRAW X1,Y1
460     X2=XC+(RADIUS/2)*COS(POINT(I))
470     Y2=YC+(RADIUS/2)*SIN(POINT(I))
472     DISP=LEN(H$(I))+15
475     MOVE X2,Y2
480   FILL N
482     IF X2<XC THEN DISP=DISP+10
485     MOVE X2-DISP,Y2
487     PRINT H$(I);
490 NEXT I
```

You should find PIE quite easy to follow, but two points should be noted. Firstly, the program makes use of the CPC664 F I L L command. CPC464 owners do not have this command, and so no pie filling is easily possible. The second point concerns text placement (lines 460-487). Text is positioned on the graphics screen using the T A G command to tie it to the graphics cursor position. The normal start position for each text string is on the radial line bisecting the given segment, half way between the circle centre and the circumference. If the sector is on the left hand side of the circle, a displacement of the left to ten units is made.

Note the form of the data in the program. The raw data is entered into array S, with the segment title going into array H$. The angles are then worked out and these are entered into a new array CUM. CUM (short for cumulative) holds the total angle for each segment FROM 0 DEGREES. If the first three segment angles were 15 degrees, 15 degrees and five degrees, they would be represented

MAIN EURO CAR MARKET COMPETITORS 1982

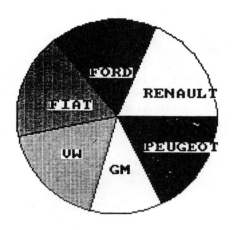

Figure 5.1 A pie chart drawn using the PIE program: MODE 1 used.

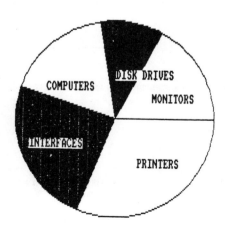

Figure 5.2 A pie chart drawn using the PIE program: MODE 2 used.

in the CUM array as 15, 30 and 35 degrees respectively. The array POINT holds
the bisected angle for the current segment, used for text plotting.

There are several variations on the pie chart theme. The first of these is called
an exploded pie chart (Figure 5.3). This is used if emphasis is to be made of a
particular segment of the pie. The logic of the EXPLODE program below is
similar to the PIE program, but extra sections to handle the exploded section are
needed. In particular, the line bisecting the exploded segment has to be found,
and the centre of the circle must temporarily be shifted along this line by the
required amount.

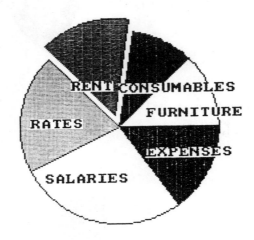

Figure 5.3 A pie chart with one segment exploded (program EXPLODE).

EXPLODE program

```
10 REM **** PROGRAM EXPLODE ****
20 REM DRAWS A LABELLED PIE CHART USING FOUR COLOURS IN MODE 1
22 REM WITH AN EXPLODED SECTION CHOSEN BY THE USER
30 REM INPUT DATA
40    CLS:INK 0,13:INK 1,0:INK 2,6:INK 3,12
50    MODE 1
60    PRINT"    WELCOME TO THE PIE CHART PROGRAM"
70    INPUT"HOW MANY SEGMENTS FOR DISPLAY?";NUMBER
80    INPUT"SEGMENT NO TO BE EXPLODED?";EXPLODE
90 IF EXPLODE=NUMBER THEN PRINT"CANNOT EXPLODE LAST SEGMENT: RESTART":GOTO 80
100 DIM S(NUMBER),H$(NUMBER),POINT(NUMBER),CUM(NUMBER)
```

```
110    TOTAL=0:CANGLE=0
120    FOR I=1 TO NUMBER
130      PRINT"INPUT TITLE FOR SEGMENT";I;:INPUT H$(I)
140      INPUT"INPUT SEGMENT VALUE";S(I)
150      TOTAL=TOTAL+S(I)
160    NEXT I
170 TAG
180    FOR I=1 TO NUMBER:REM SET ANGLES FOR EACH SEGMENT
190      CANGLE=CANGLE+((S(I)/TOTAL)*(2*PI))
200      POINT(I)=CANGLE-(((S(I)/2)/TOTAL)*(2*PI))
210      CUM(I)=CANGLE
220    NEXT I
230 CLS
240 REM SET CIRCLE SIZE
250    RADIUS=150
260    XC=320:YC=200
270    A=(2*PI)/300
280    ANGLE=0
290    X2=XC+RADIUS:Y2=YC
300    FL1=0:FL2=0:REM SET EXPLODE SEGMENT FLAGS
310    FOR I=1 TO 300
320      ANGLE=ANGLE+A
330      X1=X2:Y1=Y2
340      IF ANGLE>=CUM(EXPLODE-1)AND FL1=0 THEN GOSUB 630:REM SHIFT OUT SEGMENT
350      IF ANGLE>=CUM(EXPLODE)AND FL2=0 THEN MOVE XC,YC:DRAW X1,Y1
360      IF ANGLE>=CUM(EXPLODE)AND FL2=0 THEN XC=XHOLD:YC=YHOLD
370      X2=XC+RADIUS*COS(ANGLE)
380      Y2=YC+RADIUS*SIN(ANGLE)
390      IF ANGLE>=CUM(EXPLODE-1)AND FL1=0 THEN X1=X2:Y1=Y2
400      IF ANGLE>=CUM(EXPLODE-1)AND FL1=0 THEN MOVE XC,YC:DRAW X2,Y2:FL1=1
410 IF ANGLE>=CUM(EXPLODE) AND FL2=0 THEN ANGLE=ANGLE-A:X1=X2:Y1=Y2:FL2=1:GOTO 330
420      MOVE X1,Y1
430      DRAW X2,Y2
440    NEXT I
450 REM NOW PLOT SEGMENTS
460    N=-1
470    FOR I=1 TO NUMBER
480      N=N+1:IF N=4 THEN N=0
490      MOVE XC,YC
500      X1=XC+RADIUS*COS(CUM(I))
510      Y1=YC+RADIUS*SIN(CUM(I))
520      DRAW X1,Y1
530      X2=XC+(RADIUS/2)*COS(POINT(I))
540      Y2=YC+(RADIUS/2)*SIN(POINT(I))
550      DISP=LEN(H$(I))*3
560      MOVE X2,Y2
570      FILL N
580      IF X2<XC THEN DISP=DISP*4
590      MOVE X2-DISP,Y2
600    NEXT I
610 GOSUB 700:REM DO TITLES
615 !COPY
620 END
630 REM CALCULATE XC,YC POSITIONS FOR EXPLODED SECTION
```

```
640 REM FIRST CALCULATE BISECTION ANGLE
650     BIS = ((CUM(EXPLODE)-CUM(EXPLODE-1))/2)+CUM(EXPLODE-1)
660     XHOLD=XC:YHOLD=YC:REM STORE NORMAL CENTRE VALUES
670     XC=XHOLD+20*COS(BIS)
680     YC=YHOLD+20*SIN(BIS)
690 RETURN
700 REM NOW PLOT TITLES
710     N=-1
720     FOR I=1 TO NUMBER
730         N=N+1:IF N=4 THEN N=0
740         MOVE XC,YC
750         X1=XC+RADIUS*COS(CUM(I))
760         Y1=YC+RADIUS*SIN(CUM(I))
770         DRAW X1,Y1
780         X2=XC+(RADIUS/2)*COS(POINT(I))
790         Y2=YC+(RADIUS/2)*SIN(POINT(I))
800         DISP=LEN(H$(I))*3
810         MOVE X2,Y2
820         IF X2<XC THEN DISP=DISP*4
830         MOVE X2-DISP,Y2
840         PRINT H$(I);
850     NEXT I
870 RETURN
```

The last variation of the pie is the display of a number of 'minipies' at the same time to illustrate more complex data, for example proportional fluctuations over a period of time. As with EXPLODE, there are no real differences over the main PIE theme, but problems of placement occur. In the example below (MINIPIE), 12 small pies are shown, demonstrating differences over a twelve month period. You will see that the twelve pies are all drawn using exactly the same block of the program (lines 220-660), and only one line (line 320) is necessary to change the position of the pie to be drawn. As so much data is crammed on screen (in **MODE 2**), the data is entered in the program itself rather than interactively from the keyboard. You could of course use an input data file from tape or disk if you so wish. The cramming has also entailed the use of single letter labels. Unfortunately, **MODE 2** mean no colour, but the output looks terrible in **MODE 1 :** try it and see!

MINIPIE program

```
10 REM **** PROGRAM MINIPIE ****
20 REM THIS MODIFICATION DRAWS 12 MINI PIES COMPARING PERFORMANCE
30 REM OVER A TWELVE MONTH PERIOD.  USE ONE LETTER CODES TO LABEL PIES
40 REM MODE 2 USED FOR HIGH DEFINITION.
50 REM INPUT DATA
60     CLS:INK 0,13:INK 1,0
```

```
70   MODE 2
80 PRINT"           RELATIVE SALES OF PRODUCT LINES A-E OVER A TWELVE MONTH PERIOD"
90   READ NUMBER
100  DIM S(NUMBER,12),H$(NUMBER),POINT(NUMBER,12),CUM(NUMBER,12),TOTAL(12)
110  TOTAL=0:CANGLE=0
120  FOR I=1 TO NUMBER
130   READ H$(I)
140   REM DATA IS AT THE END OF THE PROGRAM IN THE SEQUENCE
150   REM NO OF SEGMENTS, THEN TITLE CODE, SEGMENT VALUES - FOR EACH SEGMENT
160  NEXT I
170  FOR I=1 TO 12
180    FOR IP=1 TO NUMBER
190     READ S(IP,I):TOTAL(I)=TOTAL(I)+S(IP,I):NEXT IP:NEXT I
200  GOSUB 680:REM PLOT MONTHS
210  TAG
220 REM NOW DRAW THE TWELVE PIES
230  XC=0:YC=319:REM CENTRE POINT FOR FIRST PIE
240  FOR IP=1 TO 12:REM START LOOP FOR 12 PIES
250  FOR I=1 TO NUMBER:REM SET ANGLES FOR EACH SEGMENT
260  CANGLE=CANGLE+((S(I,IP)/TOTAL(IP))*(2*PI))
270  POINT(I,IP)=CANGLE-(((S(I,IP)/2)/TOTAL(IP))*(2*PI))
280  CUM(I,IP)=CANGLE
290  NEXT I
300 REM SET CIRCLE SIZE
310  RADIUS=45
320  XC=XC+127:IF XC>=605 THEN XC=125:YC=YC-110:REM START NEW ROW
330  A=(2*PI)/100
340  ANGLE=0
350  X2=XC+RADIUS:Y2=YC
360  FOR I=1 TO 103
370    ANGLE=ANGLE+A
380    X1=X2:Y1=Y2
390    X2=XC+RADIUS*COS(ANGLE)
400    Y2=YC+RADIUS*SIN(ANGLE)
410    MOVE X1,Y1
420    DRAW X2,Y2
430  NEXT I
440 REM NOW PLOT SEGMENT
450  N=-1
460  FOR I=1 TO NUMBER
470    N=N+1:IF N=4 THEN N=0
480    MOVE XC,YC
490    X1=XC+RADIUS*COS(CUM(I,IP))
500    Y1=YC+RADIUS*SIN(CUM(I,IP))
510    DRAW X1,Y1
520    X2=XC+(RADIUS/2)*COS(POINT(I,IP))
530    Y2=YC+(RADIUS/2)*SIN(POINT(I,IP))
540    MOVE X2,Y2+6
550    IF (INT(I/2))=I/2 THEN FILL 1
560  NEXT I
570 REM NOW PLOT TITLES
580  N=-1
590  FOR I=1 TO NUMBER
600    N=N+1:IF N=4 THEN N=0
```

101

```
610      X1=XC+(RADIUS/2)*COS(POINT(I,IP))
620      Y1=YC+(RADIUS/2)*SIN(POINT(I,IP))
630      MOVE X1,Y1+6
640      PRINT H$(I);
650    NEXT I
660 NEXT IP
670 !COPY:END
680 REM MONTH PLOT
690  LOCATE 9,9:PRINT"    JAN          FEB          MAR          APR"
700  LOCATE 9,16:PRINT"    MAY          JUN          JUL          AUG"
710  LOCATE 9,23:PRINT"    SEP          OCT          NOV          DEC"
720 RETURN
730 DATA 5:REM NO OF SEGMENTS
740 DATA "A","B","C","D","E"
750 DATA 20,20,20,20,20:REM JAN
760 DATA 30,10,15,40,12:REM FEB
770 DATA 10,15,30,20,10:REM MAR
780 DATA 12,12,34,12,10:REM APR
790 DATA 14,31,12,10,19:REM MAY
800 DATA 15,31,12,8,19:REM JUN
810 DATA 13,13,14,15,12:REM JUL
820 DATA 22,15,10,12,18:REM AUG
830 DATA 15,13,10,13,17:REM SEP
840 DATA 14,41,13,24,13:REM OCT
850 DATA 5,12,13,15,13:REM NOV
860 DATA 11,21,31,8,13:REM DEC
```

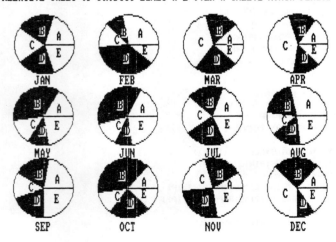

Figure 5.4 Output from MINIPIE program

5.3 Graphing techniques

The earliest form of pictorial output on a computer was probably the graph, and we are all familiar with the abstraction of numbers into a simple graph form. Graphs deal with relationships: they show the variation of one parameter with another. In the most complex cases, three or even four variables can be plotted together to produce quite complex graphs. We will only concern ourselves here with the common-or-garden two axis graph.

After your study of Chapter 1 you should already be familiar with the methods involved in the programming of a simple graph. In the present section we will consider how to improve the elementary program so that more pleasing and useful output can be produced. Here is an improved version of that earlier graph program, called SUPERG

SUPERG program

```
10 REM ****PROGRAM SUPERG****
20 REM VERSION OF GRAPH PROGRAM TO PLOT TWO VARIABLES
30 REM TO DRAW A SIMPLE LABELLED GRAPH
40     INK 0,13
50     INK 1,0
60     READ TITLE$
70     CHOICE=1:REM USE 1 FOR POINT PLOT, 2 FOR LINES
80 MODE 2
90     READ POINTS
100 DIM X(POINTS),Y(POINTS)
110     FOR I=1 TO POINTS
120 READ X(I)
130 READ Y(I)
140     NEXT I
150     READ XMIN,XMAX,YMIN,YMAX
160     READ X$:REM X AXIS NAME
170     READ Y$:REM Y AXIS NAME
180 CLS
190 REM NOW DRAW THE AXES
200        MOVE 100,380
210        DRAW 100,80
220        DRAW 550,80
230 REM PUT IN SCALE MARKS
240     FOR I=1 TO 11
250        MOVE 90,(I*30)+50
260        DRAW 100,(I*30)+50
270     NEXT I
280     FOR I=1 TO 16
290        MOVE (I*30)+70,70
300        DRAW (I*30)+70,80
```

```
310    NEXT I
320 REM PRINT TITLE
330    P1=LEN(TITLE$):P1=40-(P1/2)
340    LOCATE P1,1:PRINT TITLE$;
350 REM NOW LABEL AXES
360 REM POSITION X LABEL FIRST
370 REM START POSITION IS CENTRE PT ON X AXIS MINUS HALF STRING LENGTH
380    AX=(320-((LEN(X$)*16)/2))
390 REM START POSITION IS CENTRE PT ON Y AXIS PLUS HALF STRING LENGTH
400    AY=(220+((LEN(Y$)*16)/2))
410 TAG
420        MOVE AX,40
430    PRINT X$;
440 REM NOW PRINT Y LABEL VERTICALLY
450    FOR I=1 TO LEN(Y$):M1$=MID$(Y$,I,1)
460        MOVE 40,AY-((I-1)*16)
470    PRINT M1$;
480    NEXT I
490    MOVE 530,60:PRINT XMAX;
500    MOVE 50,382:PRINT YMAX;
510    MOVE 70,90:PRINT YMIN;
520    MOVE 80,60:PRINT XMIN;
530   MOVE 55,240:PRINT INT((YMAX+YMIN)/2);
540   MOVE 290,60:PRINT INT((XMAX+XMIN)/2);
550 REM NOW PLOT POINTS
560    IF CHOICE=2 THEN GOTO 640
570 FOR I=1 TO POINTS
580  XTOP=XMAX-XMIN:YTOP=YMAX-YMIN
590  XTRUE=XTOP-(XMAX-X(I)):YTRUE=YTOP-(YMAX-Y(I))
600     MOVE 96+(450*(XTRUE/XTOP)),86+(300*(YTRUE/YTOP))
610     PRINT CHR$(244);
620 NEXT I
630 :COPY:END
640 REM LINE PLOT SECTION
650 FOR I=1 TO POINTS
660  XTOP=XMAX-XMIN:YTOP=YMAX-YMIN
670  XTRUE=XTOP-(XMAX-X(I)):YTRUE=YTOP-(YMAX-Y(I))
680 IF I=1 THEN MOVE 96+(450*(XTRUE/XTOP)),86+(300*(YTRUE/YTOP))
690    DRAW 96+(450*(XTRUE/XTOP)),86+(300*(YTRUE/YTOP))
700 NEXT I
710 :COPY:END
720 REM DATA - IN SEQUENCE -  TITLE,NUMBER OF POINTS,XVAL YVAL FOR EACH POINT
730 REM                      XMIN, XMAX,YMIN,YMAX
740 REM                      X$,Y$
750 DATA "SHARE INDEX OVER A SIXTEEN YEAR PERIOD"
760 DATA 16,1970,380,1971,550,1972,500,1973,400,1974,270,1975,290,1976,480,1977
765 DATA 500,1978,500,1979,500,1980,495,1981,520,1982,540,1983,660,1984,800,1985,940
770 DATA 1970,1985,0,1000
780 DATA "YEAR","FT ORDINARY INDEX"
```

SUPERG uses MODE 2 to give a clean, crisp appearance. most graphs look just
as good in monochrome as in colour, so the lack of colour is no handicap here.
You will see that the minimum and maximum X and Y axis values are inputted

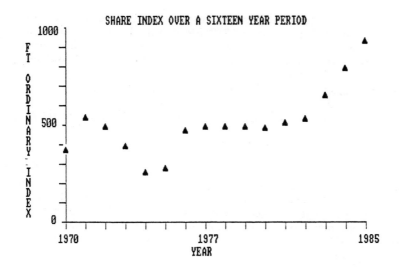

Figure 5.5 SUPERG output: point plotting

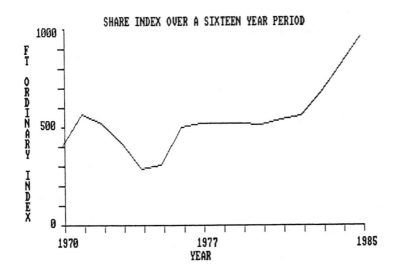

Figure 5.6 SUPERG output: line plotting

and that the program automatically scales the data into the screen coordinates using this information. The version of SUPERG given above plots each data item as an individual point. If instead you wish to plot a continuous line (Figure 5.7) a small amendment of lines 580-610 is needed. Replace lines 600-610 with

```
600  IF I=1 THEN MOVE 96+(450*(X TRUE/XTOP)),
       86+(300*(YTRUE/YTOP))
610  DRAW 96+(450*(XTRUE/XTOP)),86+(300*(YTRUE/
       YTOP))
```

Data fluctuations over a short period of time often need to be plotted. The technique in this case is more or less the same as with SUPERG, but a fancier label for the time axis is used. The following program called CHART can be used for this purpose. If your fingers are already sore from typing, let me offer some consolation: many of the programs in the rest of this chapter are variations on CHART, and you will only have to **MERGE** the alterations with the original program!

CHART program

```
10 REM **** PROGRAM CHART ****
20 REM DRAWS A LABELLED GRAPH FOR A TWELVE MONTH PERIOD
30 REM FOR EXAMPLE SALES FIGURES,CURRENCY FLUCTUATIONS, ETC
40 REM DATA IS AT END OF THE PROGRAM, BUT INTERACTIVE INPUT IS A SIMPLE CHANGE
50 DIM XP(12),YP(12)
60 CLS:MODE 2:INK 0,13:INK 1,0
70 REM INPUT LABEL INFORMATION
80    INPUT"MAIN TITLE MAX 80 CHARACTERS";T$
90    INPUT"SIDE TITLE MAX 20 CHARACTERS";S$
95    INPUT"SIDE (SUB) TITLE? MAX 20 CHARACTERS";S1$
100 REM NOW CALCULATE TITLE POSITIONS
110    T1=LEN(T$)
120    T2=LEN(S$)
125    T3=LEN(S1$)
130    XT=40-(T1/2)
140    XS=10-(T2/2)
145    XS1=10-(T3/2)
150    CLS
160    LOCATE XT,2:PRINT T$
170    LOCATE XS,12:PRINT S$
175    LOCATE XS1,13:PRINT S1$
180    GOSUB 450:REM PLACE MONTH LEGENDS ON SCREEN
190    REM NOW DRAW AXES
200       MOVE 145,365:DRAW 145,105
210       DRAW 550,105
220    REM MAKE Y AXIS GRADATIONS
```

```
230    FOR Y=362 TO 112 STEP -25
240    MOVE 142,Y:DRAW 147,Y
250    NEXT Y
260    REM NOW PLOT THE GRAPH
270 READ MXX
280    XF=131
290 TAG:MOVE 105,360:PRINT MXX;
300 MOVE 105,235:PRINT MXX/2;
310 MOVE 105,112:PRINT 0;
320    FOR I=1 TO 12
330    READ VALUE
340    VALUE=((VALUE/MXX)*250)+112
350    XF=XF+32
360    IF I=1 THEN X2=XF:Y2=VALUE
370    X1=X2:Y1=Y2
380     X2=XF:Y2=VALUE
390     MOVE X1,Y1
400      DRAW X2,Y2
420    NEXT I
430 !COPY
440 GOTO 440
450    REM MONTH LEGENDS
460 LOCATE 1,19
470    PRINT TAB(21);"!  !  !  !  !  !  !  !  !  !  !  !"
480    PRINT TAB(21);"J  F  M  A  M  J  J  A  S  O  N  D"
490    PRINT TAB(21);"A  E  A  P  A  U  U  U  E  C  O  E"
500    PRINT TAB(21);"N  B  R  R  Y  N  L  G  P  T  V  C"
510    RETURN
520 DATA 10
530 DATA 1.6,1.8,2.5,2.7,1.1,3.6,4.6,5.9,7.2,8.1,7.1,9.3
```

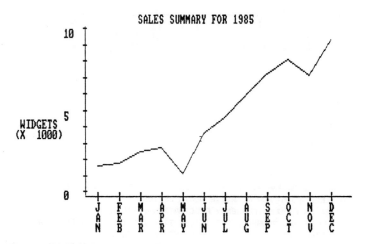

Figure 5.7 CHART output

107

The data is in the form of data statements, which are read in and plotted at lines 3320-420. This graph program illustrates variations over a twelve month period, with the months along the X axis. The Y axis legend is also printed horizontally.

It is sometimes useful to use a graph to compare two sets of data. In the simplest case, the two lines can be plotted using a simple amendment of SUPERG or CHART with lines drawn in different colours or dash patterns or with different markers, if discrete points are to be plotted. If the comparison involves some kind of competitive performance, it may be useful to emphasize the relationship between the two data lines. Figure 5.9 shows an example of this type. The periods when one of the two products was dominant are highlighted in a defined colour.

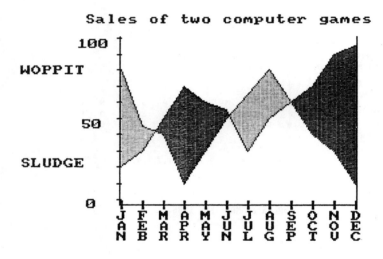

Figure 5.8 EMPHASIS output

EMPHASIS program

```
10 REM **** PROGRAM EMPHASIS ****
20 REM VERSION OF CHART PROGRAM HIGHLIGHTING COMPARISON BETWEEN TWO DATA SETS
40 REM DRAWS A LABELLED GRAPH FOR A TWELVE MONTH PERIOD
50 REM FOR EXAMPLE SALES FIGURES,CURRENCY FLUCTUATIONS, ETC
60 REM DATA IS AT END OF THE PROGRAM, BUT INTERACTIVE INPUT IS A SIMPLE CHANGE
70 REM THIS VERSION FILLS IN THE AREAS BETWEEN THE TWO SETS OF DATA
80 REM WITH A DIFFERENT COLOUR DEPEMDING ON WHICH LINE IS ABOVE THE OTHER
90 REM FILL COMMAND ONLY AVAILABLE WITH CPC664
```

```
100 REM MODE 1 USED HERE
110 DIM XP(12),YP(12),COMP(2,12):REM COMP IS TO HOLD PAIRS OF DATA POINTS
120   CLS:MODE 1:INK 0,13:INK 1,0:INK 2,2:INK 3,20
130 REM INPUT LABEL INFORMATION
140     INPUT"MAIN TITLE MAX 40 CHARACTERS";T$
150     INPUT"SIDE TITLE MAX 10 CHARACTERS";S$
160     INPUT"SIDE (SUB) TITLE? MAX 10 CHARACTERS";S1$
170 REM NOW CALCULATE TITLE POSITIONS
180     T1=LEN(T$)
190     T2=LEN(S$)
200     T3=LEN(S1$)
210     XT=20-(T1/2)
220     XS=5-(T2/2)
230     XS1=5-(T3/2)
240     CLS
250     LOCATE XT+1,1:PRINT T$
260     LOCATE XS,6:PRINT S$
270     LOCATE XS1,15:PRINT S1$
280     GOSUB 700:REM PLACE MONTH LEGENDS ON SCREEN
290     REM NOW DRAW AXES
300       MOVE 164,365:DRAW 164,105
310       DRAW 520,105
320       MOVE 520,105:DRAW 520,365
330     REM MAKE Y AXIS GRADATIONS
340     FOR Y=362 TO 112 STEP -25
350     MOVE 161,Y:DRAW 167,Y
360     NEXT Y
370     REM NOW PLOT THE FIRST LINE
380     READ MXX
390       XF=135
400       TAG:MOVE 85,360:PRINT MXX;'
410       MOVE 90,235:PRINT MXX/2;
420       MOVE 98,112:PRINT 0;
430       FOR I=1 TO 12
440       READ VALUE
450       VALUE=((VALUE/MXX)*250)+112
460       COMP(1,I)=VALUE:REM LOAD VALUE OF DATA SET POINT FOR LATER COMPARISON
470       YMIN=115
480       XF=XF+32
490       IF I=1 THEN X2=XF:Y2=VALUE
500       X1=X2:Y1=Y2
510       X2=XF:Y2=VALUE
520       MOVE X1,Y1
530       DRAW X2,Y2
540       NEXT I
550 REM NOW PLOT THE SECOND LINE
560       XF=135
570       FOR I=1 TO 12
580       READ VALUE
590       VALUE=((VALUE/MXX)*250)+112
600       COMP(2,I)=VALUE:REM LOAD VALUE OF DATA SET POINT FOR LATER COMPARISON
610       XF=XF+32
620       IF I=1 THEN X2=XF:Y2=VALUE
630       X1=X2:Y1=Y2
```

109

```
640      X2=XF:Y2=VALUE
650      MOVE X1,Y1
660      DRAW X2,Y2
670      NEXT I
680  GOSUB 800:REM FILL IN COLOURED AREAS
690  :COPY:END
700  REM MONTH LEGENDS
710  LOCATE 1,19
720  PRINT TAB(11);"! ! ! ! ! ! ! ! ! ! ! !"
730  PRINT TAB(11);"J F M A M J J A S O N D"
740  PRINT TAB(11);"A E A P A U U U E C O E"
750  PRINT TAB(11);"N B R R Y N L G P T V C"
760  RETURN
770 DATA 100
780 DATA 80,45,40,10,30,50,65,80,60,40,30,10
790 DATA 20,30,50,70,60,55,30,50,60,70,90,95
800 REM NOW FILL IN COLOURED AREAS USING FILL COMMAND
810      XX=135
820      FOR I=1 TO 12
830          IF COMP(1,I) < COMP(2,I) THEN COL=2
840          IF COMP(1,I) > COMP(2,I) THEN COL=3
850          IF COMP(1,I) = COMP(2,I) THEN XX=XX+32:GOTO 900
860          YY = (COMP(1,I)+COMP(2,I))/2
870          XX = XX+32
880          MOVE XX,YY
890          FILL COL
900      NEXT I
910 RETURN
```

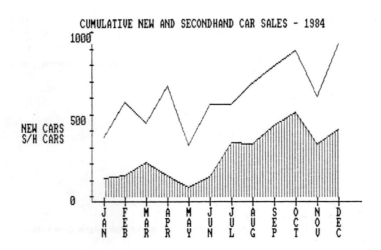

Figure 5.9 Cumulative graph drawn using CUMUL amendment of the CHART program.

110

EMPHASIS makes use of the FILL command and so will be of limited usefulness to CPC464 owners. It also uses **MODE 1**, producing rather coarse looking output.

EMPHASIS highlights the difference between two data sets. Often, however, the cumulative effect of multiple sets of data is of interest. Figure 5.9 shows an example. The bottom line here is the true line for the first data set. The top line is not the true line for the second data set but is instead the cumulative total of both sets.

To use the cumulative program CUMUL, type and save the following lines, and then **MERGE** them with CHART already in memory.

CUMUL program

```
10 REM **** PROGRAM CHART ****
12 REM CUMUL AMMENDMENT
15 YMIN=400
45 REM THIS VERSION DRAWS A CUMULATIVE GRAPH FOR TWO SETS OF DATA
46 REM LOWER DATA SET IS SHADED (ROUTINE AT LINE 1000)
260    REM NOW PLOT THE TOP GRAPH
270 READ MXX
280    XF=131
290    TAG:MOVE 105,360:PRINT MXX;
300    MOVE 105,235:PRINT MXX/2;
310    MOVE 105,112:PRINT 0;
320    FOR I=1 TO 12
330    READ VALUE
340    VALUE=((VALUE/MXX)*250)+112
345    YMIN=115
350    XF=XF+32
360    IF I=1 THEN X2=XF:Y2=VALUE
370    X1=X2:Y1=Y2
380    X2=XF:Y2=VALUE
390    MOVE X1,Y1
400    DRAW X2,Y2
420    NEXT I
422 REM NOW PLOT THE BOTTOM LINE
426    XF=131
428    FOR I=1 TO 12
430    READ VALUE
432    VALUE=((VALUE/MXX)*250)+112
434    XF=XF+32
436    IF I=1 THEN X2=XF:Y2=VALUE
438    X1=X2:Y1=Y2
439    X2=XF:Y2=VALUE
440    MOVE X1,Y1
442    DRAW X2,Y2
444    NEXT I
```

```
446    GOSUB 1000:REM FILL IN TOP AREA
448    GOTO 448
520 DATA 10
530 DATA 3.6,5.8,4.5,6.7,3.1,5.6,5.6,6.9,7.9,8.9,6.1,9.3
540 DATA 1.1,1.3,2.1,1.3,0.6,1.2,3.3,3.2,4.3,5.1,3.2,4.1
1000 REM SHADE TOP LINE VALUES
1005   INC=4
1010   YVAL=YMIN-2:REM SET SEED POSITION FOR HATCH PATTERN
1015   XX=250+INC
1020   FOR YY=YVAL TO 400 STEP 2
1030   IF TEST(XX,YY)<>0 THEN 1100
1040   PLOT XX,YY
1065   NEXT YY
1100   FOR YY=YVAL TO 0 STEP -2
1110   IF TEST(XX,YY-1)<>0 THEN 1200
1120   PLOT XX,YY
1130   NEXT YY
1200   XX=XX+INC
1210   IF XX>515 THEN INC=-INC:XX=250
1220   IF XX<165 THEN RETURN
1230   GOTO 1020
```

To the obvious relief of the CPC464 owner (and to allow MODE 2 to be used), the shaded part of the graph uses a hatching routine in the program itself (routine at line 1000). This routine moves along the X axis by a chosen increment set by INC (line 1005) and draws a line vertically upwards at each step from the Y=0 position to the point at which the vertical line hits the lower line of the graph.

5.4 Bar charts

A useful technique to aid the interpretation of data graphs is to plot the points as 'bars' instead of points. Colour or shading patterns can be used to improve the appearance of the bars. The simplest form of bar chart is demonstrated by the program BAR below. This is an amendment of the CHART program, and it should be MERGED with CHART already in memory.

BAR program

```
10 REM **** BAR CHART ADDITIONS TO PROGRAM CHART ****
20 REM DRAWS A LABELLED BAR CHART FOR A TWELVE MONTH PERIOD
260    REM NOW PLOT THE BARS
270 READ MXX
280    XF=131
290    TAG:MOVE 105,360:PRINT MXX;
```

```
300    MOVE 105,235:PRINT MXX/2;
310    MOVE 105,112:PRINT 0;
320    FOR I=1 TO 12
330    READ VALUE
340    VALUE=((VALUE/MXX)*250)+112
350    XF=XF+32
360    REM DRAW THE RECTANGLE FOR THIS MONTH
370    MOVE XF-8,VALUE:DRAW XF+8,VALUE
380    DRAW XF+8,112
390    DRAW XF-8,112
400    DRAW XF-8,VALUE
410    MOVE XF,115:FILL 1
420    NEXT I
```

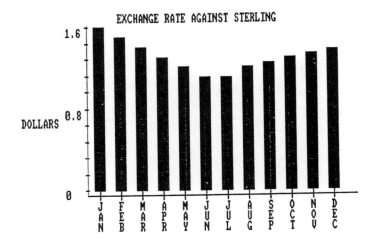

Figure 5.10 BAR output

As you can see, the changes are fairly minimal: instead of plotting a series of points, rectangles ('bars') are drawn. In BAR, the bars are coloured using the CPC664 F I L L command. CPC464 owners can either leave the bars empty, or consider using a hatched pattern to fill each bar. Here is a simple program PATTERN that enables you to fill rectangles with a variety of possible hatched patterns (Figure 5.11

PATTERN program

```
10 REM RECTANGLE HATCH TEST PROGRAM
20 CLS
25 LOCATE 12,2:PRINT"    EXAMPLES OF RECTANGLE FILL PATTERNS FOR BAR CHARTS"
30 READ XL,XR,YB,YT
35 READ XA,YA,SEP
40 IF XL=1 THEN !COPY:END
1020    MOVE XL,YT
1030    DRAW XL,YB
1040    DRAW XR,YB
1050    DRAW XR,YT
1060    DRAW XL,YT
1080 REM FIRST FILL IN UPPER SECTION
1085 IF XA/YA>2 THEN 1165
1090    FOR L= XR TO XL STEP -SEP * 3
1100       X=L
1110       Y=YT
1120       PLOT X,Y
1130       X=X-XA
1140       Y=Y-YA
1150       IF Y>=YB AND X>XL THEN  1120
1160    NEXT L
1165 IF YA/XA>2 THEN 1260
1170 REM NOW FILL IN LOWER SECTION
1180    FOR L= YT TO YB STEP -SEP * 3
1190       Y=L
1200       X=XR
1210       PLOT X,Y
1220       Y=Y-YA
1230       X=X-XA
1240       IF Y>=YB AND X>XL THEN 1210
1250    NEXT L
1260 GOTO 30
2000 DATA 100,150,300,350,1,1,2
2010 DATA 200,250,300,350,1,1,4
2020 DATA 300,350,300,350,1,1,6
2030 DATA 400,450,300,350,4,4,2
2040 DATA 500,550,300,350,4,4,4
2050 DATA 100,150,200,250,4,4,6
2060 DATA 200,250,200,250,8,8,2
2070 DATA 300,350,200,250,8,8,4
2080 DATA 400,450,200,250,8,8,6
2090 DATA 500,550,200,250,1,8,3
2100 DATA 100,150,100,150,1,8,1
2110 DATA 200,250,100,150,1,8,2
2120 DATA 300,350,100,150,8,1,4
2130 DATA 400,450,100,150,3,5,4
2140 DATA 500,550,100,150,6,2,4
2145 DATA 1,1,1,1,1,1,1
```

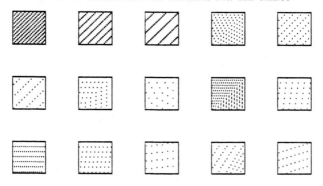

Figure 5.11 Hatching patterns produced using PATTERN program.

PATTERN generates the output shown in Figure 5.11. To use the method with a bar chart program you will need the section between lines 1080 and 1250 as a subroutine in your program. For example in BAR you would substitute the command F I L L 1 with G O S U B 5 0 0 0, putting the PATTERN section from lines 5000 onwards, Before calling this subroutine, set XL,XR,YB,YT to equal the four corners of the bar. XA, YA and SEP should be set to give the required fill pattern. The following version of BAR called HATCH demonstrates the complete procedure. Again, merge it with CHART in memory.

HATCH program

```
405    XL=XF-8:XR=XF+8:YT=VALUE:YB=115:REM LOAD CORNERS FOR HATCH
410    MOVE XF,115:GOSUB 5000:REM HATCH
5000 REM SUBROUTINE HATCH: MERGE WITH CHART+BAR
5005 XA=1:YA=1:SEP=2:REM SET HATCH VALUES
5010 IF XA/YA>2 THEN 5100
5020   FOR L= XR TO XL STEP -SEP * 3
5030     X=L
5040     Y=YT
5050     PLOT X,Y
5060     X=X-XA
5070     Y=Y-YA
5080     IF Y>=YB AND X>XL THEN  5050
5090   NEXT L
5100 IF YA/XA>2 THEN RETURN
5110 REM NOW FILL IN LOWER SECTION
```

```
5120    FOR L= YT TO YB STEP -SEP * 3
5130       Y=L
5140       X=XR
5150       PLOT X,Y
5160       Y=Y-YA
5170       X=X-XA
5180       IF Y>=YB AND X>XL THEN 5150
5190    NEXT L
5200 RETURN
```

Hatching or colouring becomes important if you wish to use a bar chart for comparative or cumulative display of several sets of data. Figure 5.13 shows a comparative method. Again, the CHART basic program is used, but instead of the BAR changes, the following amendments should be used.

BARCOMP program

```
10 REM **** BARCOMP - BAR CHART ADDITIONS TO PROGRAM CHART ****
20 REM DRAWS A BAR CHART WITH TWO SETS OF DATA FOR COMPARISONS
25 REM 2 DATA POINTS FOR EACH MONTH READ TOGETHER
260    REM NOW PLOT THE BARS
265 READ MXX
270    XF=129
275    TAG:MOVE 105,360:PRINT MXX;
280    MOVE 105,235:PRINT MXX/2;
285    MOVE 105,112:PRINT 0;
290    FOR I=1 TO 12
295    READ VALUE
300    VALUE=((VALUE/MXX)*250)+112
305    XF=XF+32
310    REM NOW DRAW THE FIRST RECTANGLE
315    MOVE XF-8,VALUE:DRAW XF+8,VALUE
320    DRAW XF+8,112
325    DRAW XF-8,112
330    DRAW XF-8,VALUE
335    MOVE XF,115:FILL 1
340    REM NOW DRAW THE SECOND RECTANGLE FOR THIS MONTH
345    READ VALUE
350    VALUE=((VALUE/MXX)*250)+112
355    XF=XF+6
360    REM DISPLACED BY 6 PIXELS FROM FIRST RECTANGLE
365    MOVE XF-8,VALUE:DRAW XF+8,VALUE
370    DRAW XF+8,112
375    DRAW XF-8,112
380    DRAW XF-8,VALUE
385    XF=XF-6
390    NEXT I
400 REM OVERWRITE THIS LINE
```

```
420 REM OVERWRITE THIS LINE
520 DATA 100
530 DATA 50,40, 60,20, 70,10, 65,45, 45,75, 10,67
540 DATA 40,75, 50,50, 60,23, 56,43, 45,67, 54,10
```

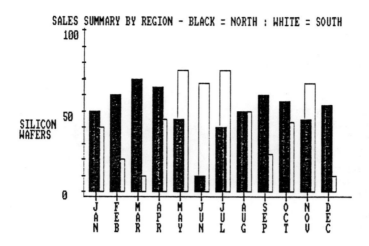

Figure 5.12 Two sets of bar chart data plotted on the same axes using the BARCOMP amendments to program BAR.

As before, this code should be merged with CHART already in memory. You can use HATCH with this program if you wish.

5.5 3D bar charts

It is also possible to draw a 'three dimensional bar chart' to look at the behaviour of three variables simultaneously. The HISTO3D program below allows you to do this, and typical output from the program is shown in Figures 5.13 and 5.14. This program is not a 'real' three dimensional program, as it cheats by incrementing the X and Y axes to give a 3D effect.

HIST03D program

```
10 REM ****HISTO3D ****
20    CLS
30    MODE 1:INK 0,13:INK 1,0:INK 2,9:INK 3,15
40    REM DRAW BACKGROUND
```

```
50      GRAPHICS PEN 1
60      X=460:XL=40:XR=639
70      MOVE X,400
80      DRAW X,160
90      MOVE XL,340
100     DRAW XL,100
110     MOVE XR,340
120     DRAW XR,100
130     A=1000
140     RW=4
150     C$="E"
160     FOR Y=400 TO 160 STEP -(160/6)
170       MOVE X,Y
180       MASK 16
190       DRAW XL,Y-60
200       IF C$="O"THEN 270
210       LOCATE 2,RW
220       PRINT A;
230       C$="O"
240       A=A-250
250       RW=RW+3.7
260       GOTO 280
270       C$="E"
280       MOVE X,Y
290       DRAW XR,Y-60
300     NEXT Y
310     MOVE 40,100
320     DRAW 220,40
330     DRAW 639,100
340     MASK 255
350       LOCATE 17,23:PRINT"1970";
360       LOCATE 26,22:PRINT"1975";
370       LOCATE 35,21:PRINT"1980";
380 H=40:C=0
390 XL=80
400 YL=100
410 XS=240
420 MR=-50/210
430 ML=15/89
440 F=3:O=2
450 H=100
460 REM NOW DO THE BLOCKS
470 GRAPHICS PEN F
480     FOR X=XS TO XS+20
490     MOVE X,20
500     DRAW X,1
510     NEXT X
515 LOCATE 5,25:PRINT"FRANCE"
516 LOCATE 21,25:PRINT" W GERMANY"
520       FOR J=1 TO 3
530       READ DA:REM GET DATA
540       TP=(240*DA)/900
550       GOSUB 680:REM COLOUR BARS
560       GOSUB 980:REM OUTLINE BARS
```

118

```
570        XL=XL+146
580        YL=YL+20:REM STEP BARS
590        NEXT J
600  C=C+1
605  LOCATE 1,1
610  IF C=2 THEN END
620      XL=182
630      YL=75:REM STEP BARS FOR NEXT ROW
640      F=2
650      O=3
660      XS=544
670  GOTO 460
680  REM FILL IN BOX
690        BL=YL+TP-ML*XL
700        BR=YL-MR*XL
710        FOR X=XL TO XL+H/2
720            Y1=ML*X+BL
730            Y2=MR*X+BR
740            GRAPHICS PEN F
750            MOVE X,Y1
760            DRAW X,Y2
770            GRAPHICS PEN 1
780            PLOT X,Y1
790            PLOT X,Y2
800        NEXT X
810      YT=Y1
820      YB=Y2
830        BL=YB-ML*(XL+H/2)
840        BR=YT-MR*(XL+H/2)
860            Y1=MR*X+BR
870            Y2=ML*X+BL
880            GRAPHICS PEN F
890            MOVE X,Y1
900            DRAW X,Y2
910            GRAPHICS PEN 1
920            PLOT X,Y1
930            PLOT X,Y2
940        NEXT X
950      YR=Y2
960      RETURN
970  REM BAR OUTLINE ROUTINE
980      MOVE XL,YL
990      GRAPHICS PEN 1
1000     DRAW XL,YL+TP
1010     MOVE XL+H/2,YB
1020     DRAW XL+H/2,YB+TP
1030     MOVE XL+H,YR
1040     DRAW XL+H,YR+TP
1050     MOVE XL+H/2,YB+TP
1060     DRAW XL+H,YR+TP
1070     MOVE XL,YL+TP
1080     DRAW XL+H/2,YR+TP-(6*(H/80))
1090 RETURN
1100 DATA 500,500,750,250,500,750
```

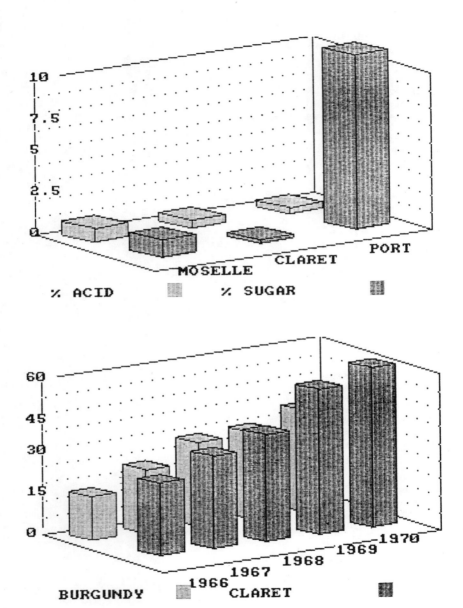

Figure 5.13, 5.14 Output from HISTO3D. Data from the 'World Atlas of Wine' by Hugh Johnson (Mitchell Beazley)

Here is the outline of HISTO3D

LINE 10- 50   SET COLOURS, MODE CLEAR SCREEN
      60-340   DRAW GRID
     350-370   PLOT X AXIS SCALE
     380-450   SET VARIABLES
               H=WIDTH OF BARS
               MR, ML=X AND Y SLOPES
               F,O=INK MODES FOR PLOTTING
               XL,YL=LOWER LEFT POINT OF BAR
               XS=POSITION OF COLOUR CODE BLOCKS
     460-510   PLOT COLOUR CODE BLOCKS
     515-516   PLOT COLOUR CODE LEGENDS
     520-670   MAIN LOOP
     600   INCREMENT ROW COUNTER
     605   PUT TEXT CURSOR AT HOME POSITION
     610   TEST IF ALL ROWS DONE
     620-660   SET VARIABLES FOR NEXT ROW
     670   END OF MAIN LOOP
     680-960   ROUTINE TO FILL BAR WITH COLOUR
               BL,BR=Y VALUES FOR LEFT EDGES OF BAR
     970- 1090 ROUTINE TO OUTLINE BAR
     1100   DATA (FOR EACH ROW IN LEFT-RIGHT ORDER)

Once the heights of the bars have been set, the routines at lines 680 and 970 fill in and outline the bars for each data point. As the rear bars are drawn first, a 'hidden surface' effect (see Chapter 8) is given, because the front bars overlap those drawn previously.

The CPC664 **MASK** command is used in lines 180 and 340 to draw the outline grid. If you have a CPC464 you could use the DASH program (Chapter 2) to draw dotted lines, or alternatively the lines can be drawn unbroken if required. The **MASK** value can of course be changed if required.

There are many other variations on the business graphics methods that we have not considered in this chapter. You can, for example display a pie chart and a graph at the same time, or plot two bar charts simultaneously, one extending up the Y axis, one extending down it. I leave these and other variations for you to program: the methods are based on the principles that we have already looked at.

Chapter 6

A Computer-Aided Design Program

6.1 Design considerations

Most of the material that we have so far considered provides useful groundwork for the manipulation of two dimensional images on the computer screen. Apart from the business area, we have not yet looked at 'serious' uses of 2D graphics, and although I hinted at the limitations of BASIC for a number of graphics application?time for us to roll up our sleeves and see just what we can create.

Computer graphics are extensively used in the professional world for computer-aided design work (CAD), where complex structures may be designed by building up pictures or diagrams from a number of subcomponents. These subcomponents may in turn be manipulated on screen to change and update the structure being designed. We have already met the geometrical transformations that act as the raw materials required to implement a simplified version of a design package on a microcomputer, and the problem that remains is how to put the components together into a coherent program. This problem really distills down to the complexity of the data structures which hold the elements used in the picture.

The program package, which we will naturally enough call DESIGN, is flexible enough to require little modification to design floor plans of houses, furniture layouts, weather maps, anything in fact where you wish to spatially design things in two dimensions. The opportunities for customising will become clearer as the program unfolds itself.

6.2 Some nuts and bolts

Let us first decide on a simple set of picture elements which should be included in a design package of this type. First and foremost, we need a basic outline of the object to be designed. We will assume for the present purpose that each object is a space enclosed by a series of points: a polygon or series of polygons, if you want to be geometrical.

We can now review our armoury of techniques to see just what we have at our disposal (and what we wish to achieve with the DESIGN program). Our major ally will be the routines in the program SKETCH, and the 'line dragging' method will be used to draw the outline and major demarcations within the system. The smaller elements which will be positioned at various points over the outline will also be separately defined using SKETCH routines, but a combination of 2D transformations will be used to simplify drawing and recall of the elements. The coordinates of each element will be stored in our old friends the X and Y coordinate arrays, and the W array will perform the same purpose as always, namely to orchestrate connection of coordinate pairs by lines.

The major sophistication in the data structures used in DESIGN is the S array which, you will recall from Chapter 3, is used to keep track of the various segments that may be in use). If you look back to section 2 of Chapter 2, you'll see that we defined S as a 2 X n array, where n is the number of segments. DESIGN uses the first segment to represent the outline of the structure on which the design is to be carried out, in this case the boundary and major demarcations. The other segments are used for the various items to be placed on the design area.

Besides keeping track of the shapes and sizes of the various segments which are manipulated on screen, the positions of the segments must be recorded. You will remember from Chapter 3 that the four chairs in the simple segment demonstration picture are in fact the same segment repeated four times. None of the data structures that we have looked at so far give any information for reconstructing multiple appearances of segments, or indeed, allow segments to be displayed at different points on screen. A new array, dimensioned RD(3,i) is used for this purpose in the DESIGN program. In this case i represents the total number of items in the picture (each appearance of a segment counts as an extra item), and for each item the X and Y coordinates of the centre point of the item, together with the segment number of the item, are recorded. So for a picture containing five items chosen from three segments, the RD array might appear as follows:

X	Y	segment no.
140	100	3
100	80	1
120	10	1
200	60	2
200	130	2

As you will see as we build up the DESIGN program, the data structures that we now have at our disposal (X, Y, W, S, and RD) allow complex pictures to be constructed and manipulated.

The RD array allows items to be positioned on screen using only one pair of coordinate points. How is this possible? Unlike the segment data considered in the original SKETCH program, the DESIGN segment data is translated to the origin as soon as it has been created. This is accomplished using essentially the same method as was introduced in Chapter 4: the centre point within the segment is calculated, and all coordinate points within the segment have their values decreased by the X or Y value of the centre point. This effectively positions the centre point at position 0,0, with the other points around it. In order to centre the translated segment 'neatly' around the origin, the midpoints between minimum and maximum X and Y values are set as the centre point to be translated to the origin. Note that there need not be a physical point at this midpoint, as it is only used as a reference point.

When a segment is to be recalled on screen, it can be drawn around any given X,Y point by merely translating all X and Y coordinates in the stored segment data by +X and +Y.

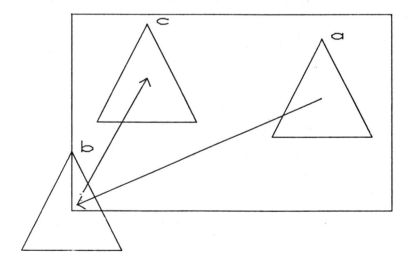

Figure 6.1 Segment creation and translation. A segment may be drawn at any point on the screen and then translated by -X, -Y to the origin. The segment can then be redrawn around any point X1, Y1 on the screen by adding X1, Y1 to all coordinate values of the segment at the origin.

Now that we have considered the data structures used in DESIGN, the control structure of the program can be considered. Because of the complexity of DESIGN, it is not feasible to use a small set of memorised instructions to drive the program, as we did with SKETCH. We may wish to save or load files, or parts of files, to define segments or to draw outlines. In order to control the flow between these various states, a system of menus is used. You will be familiar with menu-driven software in various guises, and DESIGN uses two simple menus. The first allows selection of the main functions available within the program. A second menu offers various file load options. Here are the two menus as displayed by the program:

```
DESIGN - MAIN MENU

DRAW OUTLINE OF IMAGE     - 1
DEFINE ITEMS             - 2
SAVE PICTURE             - 3
SAVE ITEMS ONLY          - 4
LOAD PICTURE             - 5
PLOT ITEMS ON OUTLINE    - 6
WIPE ITEMS BEFORE PLOT   - 7
PRINT PICTURE            - 8
EXIT FROM PROGRAM        - 9
```

Figure 6.2 The main DESIGN menu

```
DESIGN - LOAD MENU

LOAD OUTLINE ONLY        - 1
LOAD ITEMS ONLY          - 2
LOAD OUTLINE + ITEMS     - 3
LOAD WHOLE PICTURE       - 4
```

Figure 6.3 The DESIGN load menu

Most of the options available from these two menus are contained within subroutines or groups of subroutines. This modular approach allows the construction of a flow diagram of the DESIGN program. This diagram is shown below

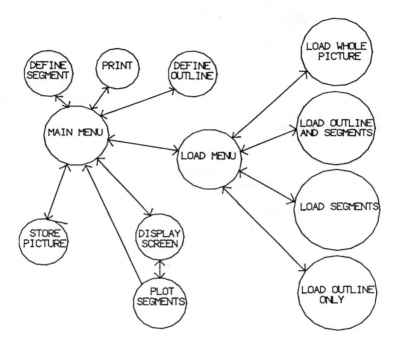

Figure 6.4 A simple flow diagram of the DESIGN program. All the options are controlled from the two menus.

As you can see from this diagram, the main functions of DESIGN are:

(1)   Menu display
(2)   Definition of segments
(3)   Definition of outline
(4)   Plotting of segments on the outline
(5)   Saving data
(6)   Loading data
(7)   Printout of picture

In order to perform these functions, a number of technical details have to be taken care of. These technical details include:

(1)   Updating counters and variables for each data structure
(2)   Movement and plotting of the cursor and update of the current
        screen location of cursor
(3)   Segment translations and scaling
(4)   Picture construction from the available data
(5)   Non-menu driven control facilities

A full list of counters and other variables used in DESIGN can be found immediately before the program listing later in this chapter. Cursor handling routines are the same as used in the original SKETCH program. Segment translations have already been described in this section, but segment scaling requires some explanation.

As the final plotted size of some segments may be very small, it is useful to be able to define (draw) each segment at a 'comfortable' size, and then to shrink it to the required dimensions. This is done in the DESIGN program by drawing each element in an enlarged box equivalent to the small boxes on the right hand margin of the main design screen, as shown in Figures 6.5 and 6.6 below.

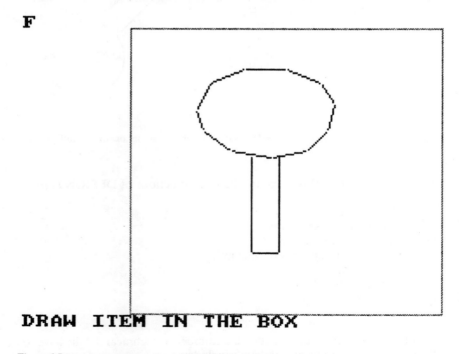

F

DRAW ITEM IN THE BOX

Figure 6.5 Drawing segment at an enlarged size in the box.

128

The picture construction methods used involve use of the RD and S arrays to access the line indices held in the W array, and ultimately the X and Y coordinates in the X and Y arrays. If item number SP is to be plotted, the X and Y coordinates of the point around which the segment is to be plotted, together with the segment type (SN), are given by the RD array, so

$$RD(1,SP)=X, \; RD(2,SP)=Y, \; RD(3,SP)=SN$$

Given this information, it is possible to access the S, W, X and Y arrays to plot segment SN around point X,Y using the following code from DESIGN.

```
FOR I = S(1,SN) TO S(2,SN)
L1 = W(1,I): L2 = W(2,I)
MOVE XP(L1)+X,YP(L1)+Y
DRAW XP(L2)+X,YP(L2)+Y
NEXT I
```

Note that the arrays XP and YP contain the coordinate data at the origin. Adding X to the XP elements and Y to the YP elements translates the segment to the correct location.

It is clearly not possible to access all functions via the menus because some control steps have to be used as the picture is being created - lines have to be initiated and terminated for example. As with SKETCH, start and stop points for newly defined lines have to be set, and recall of particular segments during the design process would be extremely tedious if the computer has to constantly switch back and forwards between the hi-res screen and the lo-res menus. As with SKETCH, some use of the keyboard is also needed (to end a segment or to signal a 'skip' within a segment). In addition, the joystick fire button is used. We will next look at the most interesting facility in computer graphics terms - the use of part of the high resolution screen itself for control purposes. This facility is only activated in design mode, where the available segments are displayed down the right hand edge of the screen. Figure 6.6 in fact shows a demonsstration of the use of the design program, and you may like to refer to it as you read on.

If the cursor is moved into one of the segment boxes, a copy of the segment may be placed anywhere on the screen merely by pressing the fire button. The segment plotted can be respecified by entering another segment box. You can also see the words 'EXIT' and 'FILL' below the segments. EXIT is self explanatory, whilst FILL causes the whole picture to be redrawn.

The use of this kind of visual representation for control purposes is becoming

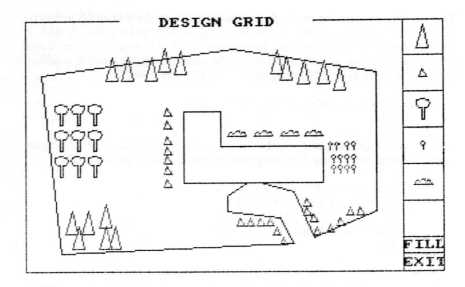

Figure 6.6 Dump of the DESIGN screen showing a 'garden' outline.

very common in areas like business graphics where the joystick-related 'mouse' is often used to move a cursor around the screen to select options available within a given program or suite of programs. It is in fact a remarkably simple technique to program. A simple test within the program checks whether or not the cursor X and Y values are within certain limits, and jumps to a different part of the program if the check is true.

6.3 The DESIGN program

Before considering the listing of DESIGN, here is the list of variables used within the program.

GENERAL FLAGS/COUNTERS

FL   flag indicating line in progress
NPTS counter for number of points within segment
NA   overall points counter
LB   overall lines counter
SE   flag for end of segment
S1   segment counter
FI   flag for line break

PF	flag for segment type (outline/item)
LI	segment line counter
S	counter for number of items plotted
CS	cursor size
SS	cursor step size
N$	name of input file
H$	name of output file
K$	character string input from keyboard
I,J	general incremental counters
PW	width of segment in pixels
WI	factor for scaling down segment width

COORDINATE VARIABLES

X	X coordinate of cursor
Y	Y coordinate of cursor
X1	temporary X coordinate values
Y1	temporary Y coordinate values
XI	X coordinate at line start
YI	Y coordinate at line start
XF	X coordinate at line finish

XH,XL maximum and minimum X values for a segment

YH,YL maximum and minimum Y values for a segment

XC,YC centre point of segment

XX,YY temporary X and Y coordinate values

ARRAYS

XP(i) arrays holding X,Y coordinate values
YP(i)

W(2,j) array holding start and finish indices for each line

S(2,k) array holding indices of first and last line in each segment

RD(3,l) array holding X and Y coordinates of each segment appearance, together with the segment type

DESIGN program

```
5 REM ****PROGRAM DESIGN****
10 REM SET CURSOR AND STEP SIZES
15 MODE 1
20 CS=2:SS=5
```

```
30 INK 0,13:INK 1,1:INK 2,3
45 CLS
50 REM NOW SET COUNTERS AND FLAGS
60 FL=0:NPTS=1:NA=1
70 LB=0:REM LINES COUNTER
80 SE=0:REM FLAG FOR SEGMENT END
90 S1=0:REM SEGMENT COUNTER
91 SP=0:REM PICTURE ELEMENT COUNTER
92 FI=0:REM FLAG FOR LINE BREAK
93 LI=0:REM SEGMENT LINE COUNTER
94 JY=1:REM LINE START/FINISH FLAG
95 PF=1: REM FLAG FOR SEGMENT TYPE
100 DIM XP(500),YP(500),LN(2,500),S(3,10),RD(3,100):REM DIMENSION ARRAYS
110 GOTO 1690:REM GOTO MAIN MENU
120 REM SET CURSOR IN CENTRE POSITION
125 IF PF=2 THEN GOSUB 2900
130 X=320:Y=200
140     GOSUB 180:REM CURSOR PLOT ROUTINE
150     GOSUB 230:REM CURSOR MOVE ROUTINE
160     GOSUB 340:REM LINE DRAG ROUTINE
170 GOTO 140
180 REM CURSOR PLOT ROUTINE
190 X1=X-CS:Y1=Y-CS:X2=X+CS:Y2=Y+CS
200     MOVE X1,Y
205     DRAW X2,Y,1,1
210     MOVE X,Y1
215     DRAW X,Y2,1,1
220 RETURN
230 REM CURSOR MOVE ROUTINE
240 Y3=Y:X3=X
250     IF JOY(0)=0 THEN 310
260     IF JOY(0)=1 THEN Y=Y+SS:GOTO 310
270     IF JOY(0)=2 THEN Y=Y-SS:GOTO 310
280     IF JOY(0)=4 THEN X=X-SS:GOTO 310
290     IF JOY(0)=8 THEN X=X+SS:GOTO 310
310         MOVE X3,Y2
320         DRAW X3,Y1,1,1
325         MOVE X1,Y3
326         DRAW X2,Y3,1,1
330 RETURN
340 REM LINE DRAG AND PLOT ROUTINE
350 A$=INKEY$
355 IF A$=""AND JOY(0)<>16 THEN IF FL=0 THEN RETURN
370 IF JOY(0)=16 AND JY=1 THEN JY=2:LOCATE 2,2:PRINT"S":GOSUB 3000:GOTO 430
380 IF JOY(0)=16 AND JY=2 THEN JY=1:LOCATE 2,2:PRINT"F":GOSUB 3000:GOTO 460
390 IF A$="B"THEN JY=1:GOTO 450:REM BREAK LINE
400 IF A$="E"THEN SE=1:JY=1:GOTO 460:REM FINISH PICTURE
420 GOTO 650:REM NORMAL LINE DRAW/WIPE
430 XI=X:YI=Y:REM START COORDINATES
440 FL=1:RETURN
450 FI=1:REM FLAG FOR LINE BREAK
460 XF=X:YF=Y:REM PUT IN POINT
480     MOVE XI,YI
485     DRAW XF,YF
```

```
490 NPTS=NPTS+1:NA=NA+1:LI=LI+1:LB=LB+1:REM INCREMENT COUNTERS
500 XP(NA)=XF:YP(NA)=YF:REM PUT IN POINTS
510 XP(NA-1)=XI:YP(NA-1)=YI:REM PUT IN POINTS
560 LN(1,LB)=NA-1:REM PUT IN LINE INDICES
570 LN(2,LB)=NA
580 IF FI=1 THEN NA=NA+1:FI=0:REM INCREMENT IF BREAK FLAG SET
590 IF SE=1 THEN S1=S1+1:S(1,S1)=NPTS-LI:S(2,S1)=NPTS-1:S(3,S1)=0:GOTO 690
630 FL=0:RETURN
640 FL=0
650 REM DO LINE DRAW/WIPE
660    MOVE X,Y
665    DRAW XI,YI,1,1
670    MOVE X,Y
675    DRAW XI,YI,1,1
680 RETURN
690 REM CONTINUE
710 FOR I=S(1,S1) TO S(2,S1)
730    MOVE XP(LN(1,I)),YP(LN(1,I))
735    DRAW XP(LN(2,I)),YP(LN(2,I)),1,0
740 NEXT I
750 K$=INKEY$:IF K$="" THEN 750
780 LI=0:FL=0:SE=0:NA=NA+1:REM YES, SO SET COUNTERS
790 IF PF=1 THEN 1690:REM OUTLINE, SO RETURN TO MAIN MENU
792 GOSUB 1000:REM SCALE DOWN PICTURE ELEMENT
794 GOTO 1690:REM RETURN TO MAIN MENU
796 GOTO 120
800 REM NOW CREATE FILE CONTAINING DATA
810 CLS
820 INPUT"OUTPUT FILENAME?";N$
830 OPENOUT N$
840 WRITE£9,NA
850 FOR I=1 TO NA
860 WRITE£9,XP(I)
870 WRITE£9,YP(I)
875 NEXT I
880 WRITE£9,LB
890 FOR I=1 TO LB
900    WRITE£9,LN(1,I)
910    WRITE£9,LN(2,I)
915 NEXT I
920    WRITE£9,S1
930 FOR I=1 TO S1
940    WRITE£9,S(1,I)
950    WRITE£9,S(2,I)
965 NEXT I
970    PRINT£9,SP
980    FOR I=1 TO SP
982       PRINT£9,RD(1,I),RD(2,I),RD(3,I)
984    NEXT I
986 CLOSEOUT
1000 REM SCALE DOWN PICTURE ELEMENT
1030 REM PRINT " SET ELEMENT SIZE:"
1040 REM INPUT " WIDTH IN PIXELS?";PW
1060 REM SET MAX AND MIN POINTERS
```

```
1070    XH=0:XL=640:YH=0:YL=400
1080    L1=LN(1,S(1,S1)):L2=LN(2,S(2,S1))
1085      FOR I=L1 TO L2
1090        IF XP(I)<XL THEN XL=XP(I)
1100        IF XP(I)>XH THEN XH=XP(I)
1110        IF YP(I)<YL THEN YL=YP(I)
1120        IF YP(I)>YH THEN YH=YP(I)
1130      NEXT I
1140 REM SET WIDTH
1145 WI=0.16
1150 REM CALCULATE CENTRE POINT FOR TRANSLATION TO ORIGIN
1160    XC=((XH+XL)/2)*WI:YC=((YH+YL)/2)*WI
1170 REM NOW SCALE DOWN OBJECT SIZE AND MOVE TO ORIGIN
1180    FOR I=L1 TO L2
1185      XP(I)=(XP(I)*WI)-XC
1186      YP(I)=(YP(I)*WI)-YC
1187    NEXT I
1190 RETURN
1200 REM POSITION SEGMENTS ON SCREEN
1210    SM=0:X=320:Y=200
1220    GOSUB 180:REM CURSOR PLOT ROUTINE
1230    GOSUB 230:REM CURSOR MOVE ROUTINE
1235      IF X>574 THEN GOSUB 1900:REM PICK SEGMENT
1240      IF JOY(0)=16 THEN GOSUB 1260:REM PLOT SEGMENT
1245      IF X<4 THEN GOTO 1690:REM RETURN TO MAIN MENU
1250    GOTO 1220:REM LOOP BACK
1260 REM PLOT SEGMENT
1265    SP=SP+1:RD(1,SP)=X:RD(2,SP)=Y:RD(3,SP)=SM
1270    FOR I=S(1,SM) TO S(2,SM)
1280      L1=LN(1,I):L2=LN(2,I)
1285          MOVE XP(L1)+X,YP(L1)+Y
1290          DRAW XP(L2)+X,YP(L2)+Y,2,0
1300    NEXT I
1310 RETURN
1330 REM FILE INPUT ROUTINE
1340 INPUT "FILENAME FOR INPUT?";H$
1360    OPENIN H$
1370    INPUT£9,NPTS
1380    FOR I=1 TO NPTS
1390      INPUT£9,XP(I),YP(I)
1395    NEXT I
1400    INPUT£9,LI
1420    FOR I=1 TO LI
1425      INPUT£9,LN(1,I),LN(2,I)
1427    NEXT I
1430    INPUT£9,S1
1440    FOR I=1 TO S1
1450      INPUT£9,S(1,I),S(2,I)
1460    NEXT I
1465    INPUT£9,SP
1470    FOR I=1 TO SP
1475      INPUT£9,RD(1,I),RD(2,I),RD(3,I)
1480    NEXT I
1485 CLOSEIN
```

```
1490 PRINT"FILE ",H$," LOADED OK"
1500 RETURN
1560 REM DESIGN BORDER DRAW ROUTINE
1570 MOVE 6,394
1575   DRAW 146,394
1580   MOVE 440,394
1590   DRAW 634,394
1600   DRAW 634,6
1610   DRAW 6,6
1620   DRAW 6,394
1630   MOVE 574,394
1635   DRAW 574,6
1640   FOR I=60 TO 340 STEP 56
1645     MOVE 574,I
1650     DRAW 634,I
1655   NEXT I
1660   MOVE 574,34
1665   DRAW 634,34
1670   LOCATE 13,1:PRINT" DESIGN GRID"
1675   IF PF=1 THEN LOCATE 1,1:PRINT"OUTLINE"
1676 RETURN
1680 REM MAIN MENU
1690 CLS:PF=2
1700 PRINT""
1710 PRINT"           DESIGN - MAIN MENU"
1720 PRINT""
1730 PRINT"     DRAW OUTLINE OF IMAGE   - 1"
1740 PRINT"     DEFINE ITEMS            - 2
1750 PRINT"     SAVE PICTURE            - 3"
1755 PRINT"     SAVE ITEMS ONLY         - 4"
1760 PRINT"     LOAD PICTURE            - 5"
1770 PRINT"     PLOT ITEMS ON OUTLINE   - 6"
1780 PRINT"     WIPE ITEMS BEFORE PLOT  - 7"
1790 PRINT"     PRINT PICTURE           - 8"
1792 PRINT"     EXIT FROM PROGRAM       - 9"
1794 K$=INKEY$: IF K$=""THEN 1794
1796    IF K$="1" THEN PF=1:CLS:GOSUB 1570:GOTO 120:REM DEFINE OUTLINE
1800    IF K$="2" THEN PF=2:CLS:GOTO 120:REM DEFINE ITEM
1810    IF K$="3" THEN GOTO 810: REM STORE ALL
1815    IF K$="4" THEN GOSUB 2700:GOTO 1680:REM STORE ITEMS ONLY
1820    IF K$="5" THEN SP=0:GOSUB 2300:GOTO 1690 :REM LOAD ALL
1830    IF K$="6" THEN CLS:GOSUB 2000:GOSUB 1570:GOSUB 2100:GOTO 1210
1840    IF K$="7" THEN CLS:SP=0:S1=1:GOSUB 2000:GOSUB 1570:GOSUB 2100:GOTO 1210
1850    IF K$="8" THEN !COPY:GOTO 1680:REM TASCOPY SCREEN DUMP
1860    IF K$="9" THEN PRINT"PROGRAM EXITED":END
1870 GOTO 1794
1900 REM SEGMENT PICK ROUTINE FOR PLOTTING
1910    IF Y>340 THEN SM=2:RETURN
1920    IF Y>284 THEN SM=3:RETURN
1930    IF Y>228 THEN SM=4:RETURN
1940    IF Y>172 THEN SM=5:RETURN
1950    IF Y>116 THEN SM=6:RETURN
1960    IF Y>60  THEN !COPY:SM=7:RETURN
1965    IF Y>32 THEN:GOSUB 2200:X=X-30:RETURN:REM RECREATE PICTURE
```

135

```
1970    IF Y<34 THEN GOTO 1690
1990    IF JOY(0)<>16 THEN RETURN
2000 REM SEGMENT PLOT ROUTINE
2010    YA=424
2020    IF S1=1 THEN 2085
2027      FOR I=2 TO S1
2030        YA=YA-56
2040        FOR J=S(1,I) TO S(2,I)
2060        MOVE XP(LN(1,J))+604,YP(LN(1,J))+YA
2065        DRAW XP(LN(2,J))+604,YP(LN(2,J))+YA,2,0
2070        NEXT J
2080      NEXT I
2082 TAG
2085 MOVE 574,54:PRINT"FILL"
2090 MOVE 574,26:PRINT"EXIT"
2092 TAGOFF
2095 RETURN
2100 REM REDRAW DESIGN OUTLINE
2110    FOR I=S(1,1) TO S(2,1)
2120      L1=LN(1,I):L2=LN(2,I)
2130      MOVE XP(L1),YP(L1)
2135      DRAW XP(L2),YP(L2),1,0
2140    NEXT I
2150 RETURN
2200 REM PICTURE RECREATE ROUTINE
2215    IF SP=0 THEN GOSUB 2100:RETURN
2220    FOR I=1 TO SP
2230      XX=RD(1,I):YY=RD(2,I)
2235      FOR J=S(1,RD(3,I)) TO S(2,RD(3,I))
2240        L1=LN(1,J):L2=LN(2,J)
2260        MOVE XP(L1)+XX,YP(L1)+YY
2265        DRAW XP(L2)+XX,YP(L2)+YY,2,0
2267      NEXT J
2270    NEXT I
2275    GOSUB 2100:REM REDRAW OUTLINE
2280 RETURN
2300 REM LOAD MENU
2310 CLS
2320 PF=2
2330 PRINT""
2340 PRINT"          DESIGN - LOAD MENU"
2350 PRINT""
2360 PRINT"     LOAD OUTLINE ONLY          - 1"
2370 PRINT"     LOAD ITEMS ONLY            - 2"
2380 PRINT"     LOAD OUTLINE + ITEMS       - 3"
2390 PRINT"     LOAD WHOLE PICTURE         - 4"
2400 K$=INKEY$:IF K$=""THEN 2400
2410    IF K$="1" THEN GOSUB 1330:NPTS=S(2,1)+1:LI=0:S1=1:NA=NPTS+1
2415    IF K$="1" THEN LB=NPTS-1:SP=0:RETURN
2420    IF K$="2" THEN GOSUB 2500:SP=0:RETURN
2425    IF K$="3" THEN GOSUB 1330:SP=0:RETURN
2430    IF K$="4" THEN GOSUB 1330:RETURN
2500 REM LOAD ITEMS ONLY
2510 INPUT"FILENAME FOR ITEMS";H$
```

136

```
2520    OPENIN H$
2530    NPTS =S(2,1)+1:LI=0:S1=1:NA=NPTS+1
2540    INPUT £9,NW
2550      FOR I=NPTS+1 TO NPTS+NW
2560        INPUT£9,XP(I),YP(I)
2570      NEXT I
2575    NPTS=NPTS+NW
2580    INPUT£9,LW
2585      FOR I=LB+1 TO LB+LW
2590        INPUT£9,LN(1,I),LN(2,I)
2595      NEXT I
2600    LB=LB+LW:LI=LB
2605    INPUT£9,S1
2610    S1=S1+1
2620      FOR I=2 TO S1
2630        INPUT£9,S(1,I),S(2,I)
2640      NEXT I
2650    PRINT"FILE ",H$," INPUTTED OK"
2655    CLOSEIN
2660    CLS
2670 RETURN
2700 REM CREATE FILE CONTAINING DATA ITEMS ONLY
2710 CLS
2720    INPUT"FILENAME FOR ITEMS";H$
2730    OPENOUT H$
2740    PRINT£9,(NA-(LN(2,S(2,1))))-1
2750      FOR I=(LN(2,S(2,1)))+1 TO NA-1
2760        PRINT£9,XP(I)
2770        PRINT£9,YP(I)
2780      NEXT I
2790    PRINT£9,LB-S(2,1)
2800 FOR I=S(2,1)+1 TO LB
2810    PRINT£9,LN(1,I)
2820    PRINT£9,LN(2,I)
2825 NEXT I
2830    PRINT£9,S1-1
2840      FOR I=2 TO S1
2850        PRINT£9,S(1,I)
2860        PRINT£9,S(2,I)
2870      NEXT I
2880    CLOSEOUT
2890 RETURN
2900 REM OUTLINE FOR SEGMENT CREATE BOX
2910 MOVE 140,368
2915 DRAW 500,368,2,0
2920 DRAW 500,32,2,0
2925 DRAW 140,32,2,0
2930 DRAW 140,368,2,0
2940 LOCATE 2,24:PRINT"DRAW ITEM IN THE BOX"
2950 RETURN
3000 FOR I=1 TO 1000:NEXT I:RETURN
```

DESIGN is used in the following way. On running the program, the main menu appears, and this allows the user to save or load files, to define segments or the outline or to print the design area. The definition options initiate 'SKETCH' mode, and a segment can be created using the joystick, fire button and keys S and E as for SKETCH. The central option is the design screen itself, which appears as below, with a given outline and available segments drawn down the right hand side of the screen. Movement of the cursor to pick up and plot individual segments is performed until the picture is complete. EXIT returns to the main menu.

The load menu allows an outline, a set of segments, or even a whole picture to be restored from disk or tape.

The DESIGN program is structured as follows

LINES	10- 20	SET UP CURSOR AND STEP SIZES
30-	45	SET UP INK COLOURS AND CLEAR SCREEN
60-	100	SET UP COUNTERS AND FLAGS
110		JUMP TO MAIN MENU DRAW ROUTINE
130		SET CURSOR IN MIDDLE OF SCREEN
125		PRINT 'SEGMENT' IF CREATING SEGMENT
140-	170	MAIN SCREEN CONTROL SECTION
180-	220	CURSOR DRAW ROUTINE
230-	330	CURSOR MOVE ROUTINE
340-	680	LINE DRAG AND PLOT SECTION
730-	790	TEST FOR END OF LINE OR SEGMENT
810-	990	CREATE DATA FILE
1000-	1190	SCALE DOWN SEGMENT SIZE
1200-	1310	POSITION SEGMENTS ON SCREEN
1320-	1550	FILE INPUT ROUTINE
1560-	1670	DRAW BORDER ROUND SCREEN
1680-	1785	MAIN MENU DISPLAY SCREEN
1790-	1850	READ KEY AND BRANCH
1900-	1910	PICK SEGMENT FOR PLOTTING
2000-	2095	PLOT SEGMENTS DOWN RH MARGIN
2100-	2160	REDRAW GARDEN OUTLINE
2200-	2300	RECREATE PICTURE ROUTINE
2310-	2390	DISPLAY LOAD MENU
2400-	2430	READ KEY FOR LOAD CHOICE AND BRANCH
2500-	2650	FILE INPUT: SEGMENTS ONLY
2700-	2880	CREATE DATA FILE (ITEMS ONLY)
3000-	3005	DELAY LOOP

These descriptions are somewhat sparse, and the following notes expand some of the more complex sections:

138

Lines 20-40

The cursor and step sizes can be altered as you wish, but of course the larger the step, the less accurate will be the final picture. A big cursor looks impressive, but remember that pixel inversion will create a lot of annoying and unnecessary 'blinking' along the cursor lines if the picture has much fine detail.

Lines 140-790

This large section is almost identical to the SKETCH program and carries out the main drawing and plotting steps.

Lines 730-790

Some differences to SKETCH are worthy of note. If the segment defined is the outline, control is immediately transferred back to the main menu. If the segment is not the outline it is scaled down (lines 1000-1190) before the main menu is accessed.

Lines 810-990

This is the main data file creation routine. All the information in the data structures is stored: outline, segment, and segment placing data are stored on disk.

Lines 1010-1190

This routine scales down a picture element drawn at large scale in the 'box'

Lines 1200-1310

Plotting segments on the screen involves three steps. First, the cursor plot and move routines are used to allow picking and placement of segments. Secondly, the segment to be plotted is picked from the options down the right hand side of the screen. The routine on lines 1900-1990 is called to handle this. The chosen segment is then plotted around the current cursor position I ines 1260-1310). The RD array is incremented and the X,Y cordinates of the current cursor position, together with the segment number, are placed in this array.

Lines 1320-1550

The main data file input routine. Data for X,Y,W,S and RD arrays are read in.

Lines 1560-1670

This routine draws the border around the screen and places the title in position. If the outline is being plotted, the word 'outline' is printed on screen.

Lines 1900-1990

The current segment number to be plotted is updated if the X position of the cursor is > 287. The cursor's Y coordinate determines the segment number. This routine is called from the segment plot routine (lines 1200-1310).

Lines 2000-2095

This routine draws the available segments down the right hand edge of the screen ready for picking in the previous routine. All segments are drawn with the same X displacement, while the Y displacement is incremented for each successive segment.

Lines 2100-2160

The outline is drawn in preparation for the plotting of the items on it.

Lines 2200-2300

This routine draws all the occurrences of every item on the screen, and is accessed by choosing the F I L L option on the plotting screen. It is used if the plotting screen is exited to define new segments, and is then reaccessed, for example.

Lines 2500-2650

This input routine assumes that an outline has already been defined, and loads in a series of segments above it into the X,Y W and S arrays. Note that the RD array is not filled by this routine, because the segment data may be used with any number of outlines and the RD information will only be specific for one outline. Note also that the outline must already exist! This is necessary to avoid the problem of how much space to leave at the beginning of the various arrays for the outline.

Lines 2700-2880

This data file creation routine does not save the outline, and the file created is used in conjunction with the previous routine.

6.4 Some applications for the DESIGN program

DESIGN has possible applications in several different areas. Figure 6.6 showed one possible use. You can create your own weather maps by drawing a map as the outline and by designing 'BBC' style weather symbols to place as you wish (will you ever need the sun symbol?). Alternatively, designs for gardens or furniture placement in a room can be made.

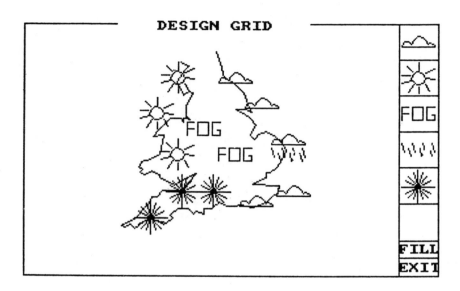

Figure 6.7 Use of the DESIGN program for drawing a weather map.

Chapter 7

Working in
Three Dimensions

7.1 Data and 2D projections

The techniques of drawing lines between points in a two dimensional plane are easy to grasp, but problems arise when we come to look at the third dimension. These problems are not specific to the CPC 6128,CPC 664 or CPC 464: they are common to all computers, although graphics software packages available on mini and mainframe computers (and some expensive micros) may include special facilities for handling three dimensional data, especially with respect to perspective and projections, topics that we will consider later in this chapter. The objects that we will look at here fall into the category of 'wire frame' pictures, because we will only be considering points and lines, not surfaces as such. The representation of solid objects will be the subject of Chapter 8.

In order to represent three dimensional data we first need to extend the rectangular coordinate system introduced in Chapter 4. Recall that in two dimensions we have an X and a Y axis extending left/right and up/down the page respectively. In three dimensions we also have to represent depth, and this is done by the use of a third axis called Z. The Z axis is conventionally drawn into/out of the page. If you stand a pencil on end on the page of a book, the pencil represents the Z axis, as you see here.

Figure 7.1 Representing the Z axis.

If the observer views the three axes from a position slightly displaced from the Z axis, the axes appear like this

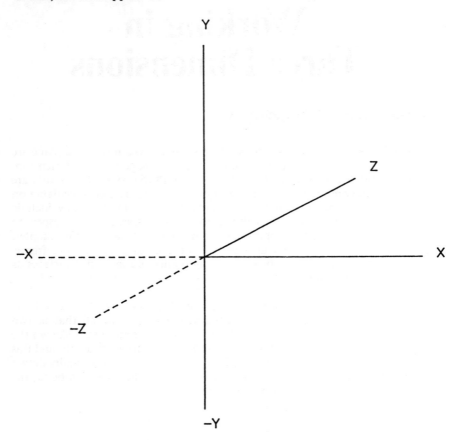

Figure 7.2 The three axes in space. The negative Z axis projects out of the screen towards the observer.

The Z data is treated in exactly the same way as the X and Y data, that is, it has its own one dimensional array set up to hold the Z coordinate data for each point. As an exercise in 'thinking three dimensionally', we can consider a cube, perhaps the simplest three dimensional object. For additional simplicity, we will also assume that the cube lies in 3D space with coordinates greater than the origin in all three dimensions. The cube will therefore be defined by a series of points, whose coordinates might then be as follows:

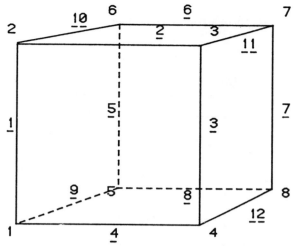

Figure 7.3 Point and line data for the cube used as a 3D example in this chapter. Line numbers are underlined.

pt no	X	Y	Z
1	50	50	50
2	50	100	50
3	100	100	50
4	100	50	50
5	50	50	100
6	50	100	100
7	100	100	100
8	100	50	100

We can also define the lines to be drawn between the points, in the same way as we did in the two dimensional case, so

i	W(1,i)	W(2,i)
1	1	2
2	2	3
3	3	4
4	4	1
5	5	6
6	6	7
7	7	8
8	8	5
9	1	5
10	2	6
11	3	7
12	4	8

Note that in this case there are more lines than points.

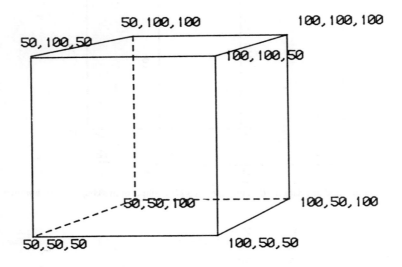

Figure 7.4 The X,Y,Z coordinates for the cube displayed in Figure 7.3.

Now the W array is dimensioned in exactly the same way in two and three dimensional representations, and it is also used in the same way. The X Y Z data on the other hand must be transformed to eliminate the Z axis before drawing, because there is no way of plotting X Y Z data on an X Y display. We cannot use the X Y Z coordinate arrays for drawing in the same way as we used the X Y data in the two dimensional case. For plotting, we will use the XP and YP arrays that have already been introduced in Chapter 3 section 3.2. The question that must now be addressed is just how we shrink down from three to two dimensions.

7.2 Projection methods

Techniques of getting from three dimensional coordinates to a 'mapping' in 2D X Y coordinate data are called projections. Look at the two diagrams below. The object that is to be projected is held in a three dimensional space called the *view volume* (analogous to the 2D window that we met in Chapter 4).

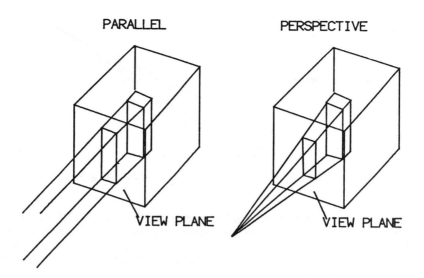

PARALLEL   PERSPECTIVE

VIEW PLANE   VIEW PLANE

Figure 7.5 Parallel and perspective views of a rectangular block within the view volume, the equivalent of the window in the two dimensional world. The view plane is the two dimensional frame on which the block is projected, and you can see that the projection is different for perspective and parallel projections.

There are two different types of projection from this volume into two dimensions, depending on the axis of projection. If projection is towards a point, we have *perspective* projection. If projection of all points in the view volume is *parallel,* then (naturally enough) the projection is called parallel. You can visualise this simply as the difference in the position of an 'observer'. If the observer is at some distance d from the view volume where d < infinity, then he will see a perspective view, as the light rays from every point on the object will converge onto his eyes. If the observer is considered to be at infinity, then the light rays will never converge, so the projection will be parallel. These railway lines show the difference between parallel and perspective views.

In general, perspective projections are more realistic, but are slightly more tricky to program. Parallel projections are conversely less 'realistic' but more straightforward. Which you use is largely a matter of the project in hand. You will be able to compare the effects of each by running the programs described in this chapter.

If you look again at the projections from the view volume shown above, you will see an element which we have still to explain. This element is the projection plane, and it holds the key to our projection problem. The projection plane is

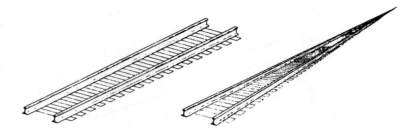

Figure 7.6 A striking example of parallel and perspective projections: railway tracks.

defined as the plane in space at which the projection lines are 'cut'. If the plane is parallel to the Z axis, the Z coordinates are lost in the plane, because all points in the plane have an identical Z value. If you compare the parallel and perspective projections, you will see that the 2D representations on the projection plane are different in each case.

So the image that is presented to the eye differs depending on the type of projection. Before looking at the mechanics of the various projection methods, we should note that the image that results from the 2D projection will vary depending on the position of the 'eye' relative to the origin. For our purposes we will assume that the eye looks straight down the Z axis, in the same kind of orientation to your eyes on the page of this book. This is not a limitation at all, because we can still rotate any 3D object around to view it from any desired position. This will become clearer when we discuss 3D transformations later on.

7.3 Entering 3D data

You will recall that we described some utilities in Chapter 3 for creating 2D data files (FILE2D, SKETCH). We have already seen that a 3D data set can be created merely by adding an extra set of Z coordinate data, and therefore FILE2D becomes FILE3D in this new version.

FILE3D program

```
10 REM ****PROGRAM FILE3D****
20 REM PROGRAM TO STORE COORDINATE DATA TO BE DRAWN
30 INPUT"FILENAME?";H$
40 OPENOUT H$
50 INPUT"NUMBER OF POINTS?";NPTS
55 WRITE£9,NPTS
```

```
60 PRINT"ENTER X,Y ,Z TRIPLETS"
70 FOR I=1 TO NPTS
80 INPUT"X=";X:INPUT"Y=";Y:INPUT"Z=";Z
90 WRITE£9,X
100 WRITE£9,Y
105 WRITE£9,Z
110 NEXT I
120 INPUT"NUMBER OF LINES?";LI
130 WRITE£9,LI
140 PRINT"ENTER NUMBERS OF JOINING POINTS"
150 FOR I=1 TO LI
160 INPUT"START NO";SN:INPUT"FINISH NO";FI
170 WRITE£9,SN
180 WRITE£9,FI
190 NEXT I
200 CLOSEOUT
210 END
```

SKETCH itself is trickier to adapt. This is not of course because there is anything inherently complex about setting up a set of 3D data points, but rather because of the difficulty of getting 'back' from the 2D projection on the screen to 3D data. This can be done in two ways. The first and 'hairiest' way is to try to define points on screen by their X Y and Z coordinates. A possible system for doing this would be to program the joystick to move the cursor around the screen in the X, Y plane as used in SKETCH. Instead of creating a 2D picture, however, two keys could be used to control movement into and out of the screen to add the Z dimension. Only when Z is set to the correct value would the line be stored as in SKETCH. The trick is of course in gauging Z. The default for Z would be set at 0, but Z could be varied from, say, -300 to $+300$. Such a system would ideally use a windowing facility at the bottom of the screen to keep you informed of the current Z value. You would have to program some kind of Z indicator onto the high resolution screen. You would also have the problem of projection to consider and the simplest solution would be to use parallel projection. It would be quite easy to amend such a program to draw in perspective, but this is of no use if you are not an artist!

After reading this last paragraph you may be excused for thinking that I have acquired the too-common syndrome seen in computer writers who describe vast numbers of juicy sounding programs without giving the code. Do not fear! The only reason that you are not faced with a program of the sort outlined here is that I really have doubts about its usefulness.

Instead, I propose a far neater, but much more restrictive program which allows you to give some depth information to your 2D data. This program, called appropriately enough SKETCH3D, allows definition of a 2D outline as in SKETCH, but after the object is drawn, Z data is added to the X,Y coordinate data. Next, data representing a second image of the outline is calculated with the same X,Y coordinates, but with Z coordinates set to a chosen value different to that of the first object image. Besides calculating the X,Y,Z coordinates in this way, the W array containing line data is also expanded to contain the lines connecting the first and second set of points. The data so far enables reconstruction of two parallel planar objects in 3D space, but this is not useful enough, because what we actually want is a single 3D object. The W array holds the key to this object, because all that is needed is a set of lines joining corresponding points in the two planes. The diagram below shows pictorially the steps in preparation of the final 3D data set. It is also possible to add additional data to the data set to enable it to be used in conjunction with a 'hidden lines' program.

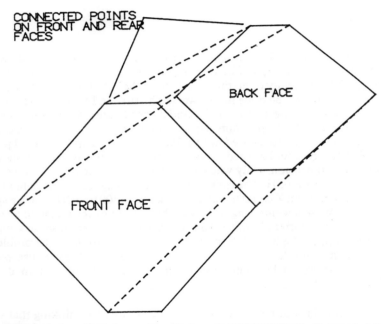

Figure 7.7 Production of a 3D data set from 2D data using SKETCH3D. The first face is defined as a series of 2D points and lines. Constant Z data are then added to each X,Y coordinate pair. The X and Y data are then duplicated to produce a back face (with Z values constant but > those of the front face). A further set of lines is set up joining corresponding points on front and back faces.

SKETCH3D is great fun to use, as it avoids calculation of streams of 3D data sets. It is of course limited to objects which benefit from the representation technique, but it is especially helpful in giving practice in 'thinking 3D'. In order to change SKETCH into SKETCH3D, MERGE the following SKETCH3D amendments with SKETCH already in your computer's memory.

SKETCH3D program

```
10 REM **** PROGRAM SKETCH3D ****
110 S(1,2)=0
800 REM NOW CREATE FILE CONTAINING DATA
810 OPENOUT N$
815 GOSUB 1200:REM GET TRANSLATION VALUES
817 PRINT "YOUR X SPREAD IS ",XH-XL
818 PRINT "YOUR Y SPREAD IS ",YH-YL
819 INPUT "INPUT YOUR Z SPREAD";ZZ
820     PRINT£9,NA*2
830     FOR I=1 TO NA
840        PRINT£9,XP(I)+XTRANS
850        PRINT£9,YP(I)+YTRANS
860        PRINT£9,-(ZZ/2)
870     NEXT I
875 REM OVERWRITE THIS LINE
880     FOR I=1 TO NA
890        PRINT£9,XP(I)+XTRANS
900        PRINT£9,YP(I)+YTRANS
910        PRINT£9,(ZZ/2)
915 REM OVERWRITE THIS LINE
920     NEXT I
930 IF S(1,2)=0 THEN S(1,2)=LB
940     PRINT£9,(2*LB)+S(1,2)-1
950     FOR I=1 TO LB
960        PRINT£9,LN(1,I),LN(2,I)
965 REM OVERWRITE THIS LINE
970     NEXT I
980     FOR I=1 TO LB
990        PRINT£9,LN(1,I)+NA
1000        PRINT£9,LN(2,I)+NA
1010     NEXT I
1020     FOR I=1 TO S(1,2)
1030        PRINT£9,I
1040        PRINT£9,I+NA
1050     NEXT I
1060     PRINT£9,S1
1070       FOR I=1 TO S1
1080          PRINT£9,S(1,I)
1090          PRINT£9,S(2,I)
1100       NEXT I
1110 CLOSEOUT
1120 END
1200 REM ROUTINE TO TRANSLATE X,Y VALS AROUND ORIGIN
1205 XL=640:YL=400:XH=0:YH=0
1210     FOR I=1 TO NA
1220        IF XP(I)<XL THEN XL=XP(I)
1230        IF XP(I)>XH THEN XH=XP(I)
1240        IF YP(I)<YL THEN YL=YP(I)
1250        IF YP(I)>YH THEN YH=YP(I)
1260     NEXT I
1270 XTRANS = -((XH+XL)/2)
```

151

```
1280 YTRANS = -((YH+YL)/2)
1290 RETURN
```

As you can see from the above code, most of the changes needed to be made to SKETCH are in the file creation section.

Line 820

The number of data points in SKETCH3D is 2*NA or twice the number drawn in the 2D picture.

Line 860

The Z coordinate values for all data points in the front face of the 3D object are arbitrarily set here at -(ZZ/2), and this can be changed as required.

Line 910

The Z coordinate values for all data points in the rear face are arbitrarily set at ZZ/2.

Line 930

The part of the front face of the object connected to the analogous points on the rear face is made up of all the points in the first segment defined. If only one segment is defined in total, the start line for the second segment will not have been set, and this will cause the program to fail on line 1020. To avoid this happening, S(1,2) is set to LB (the number of lines on the first segment) if there is only one segment present.

Line 940

The number of lines is 2* LB + S(1,2)−1. In other words, double the number of lines in the front face, plus the number of lines in the first segment defined (these are the lines connecting front and rear faces).

Lines 950-970

The first set of lines to be written to the data file are the lines on the 2D 'front surface'. These are the lines present in the SKETCH version.

Lines 980-1010

The second set of lines are the analogous lines in the rear face. These are the same as the front face lines, added to NA, the number of points in the front face.

Lines 1020-1050

The remaining lines are the connecting lines between the first segment in the front face and the corresponding points on the rear face.

Lines 1060-1100

The segment information is written to the data file.

Figure 7.8 shows the front surface of a picture created using SKETCH3D to define the data. The reconstructed 3D picture is shown in Figure 7.12.

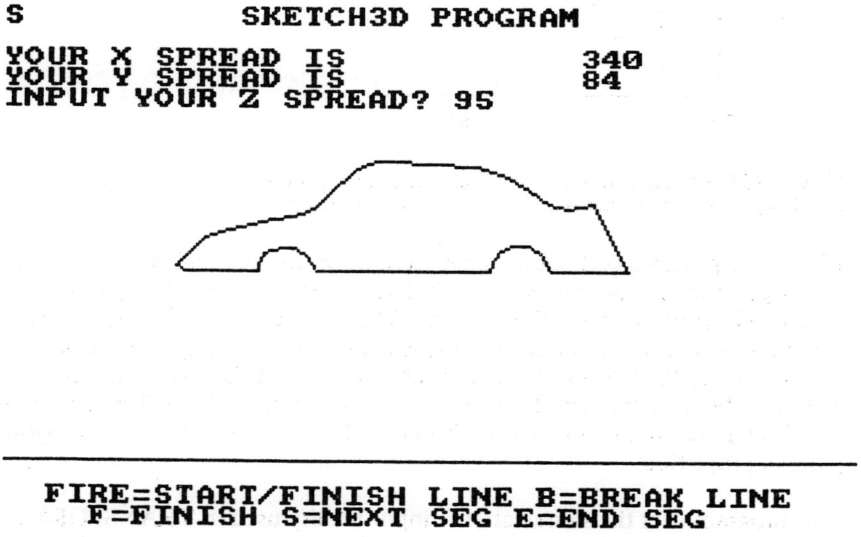

S   **SKETCH3D PROGRAM**

```
YOUR X SPREAD IS                340
YOUR Y SPREAD IS                84
INPUT YOUR Z SPREAD? 95
```

```
FIRE=START/FINISH LINE B=BREAK LINE
  F=FINISH S=NEXT SEG E=END SEG
```

Figure 7.8 Use of SKETCH3D program to create front face of a 3D image.

7.4 Parallel projections

The 'easiest' parallel projections are called orthographic projections. We are all familiar with 'front', 'side' and 'top' views of architectural plans. These are *orthographic* projections perpendicular to one of the three axes, X,Y, or Z. These views are also very boring in the case of a rectangular object that lies on the major axes because no illusion of depth is given at all!

153

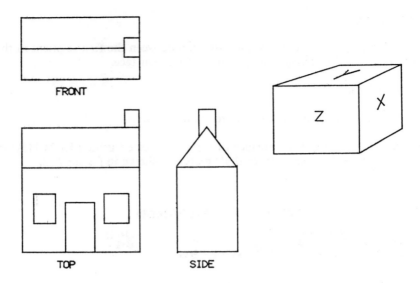

Figure 7.9 The simplest sort of projection: an architectural drawing. Front, side and top aspects of a building correspond to planes in the Z, X, and Y axes respectively.

In order to program orthographic projections of this kind, all you have to do is to 'forget' the Z axis. Any set of 3D data plotted as a 2D X,Y picture is an orthogonal projection on the Z plane. This type of program introduces the program format to handle three dimensional data setting up the various data structures (X, Y, Z, S and W arrays) needed to hold the data. The following program PROJ3D lays out the backbone for the routines that will be developed in this chapter, and can be used with any 3D data set to draw an orthogonal parallel projection.

This program uses the same data file input facility used in TRANSFORM, so if you want to use your own data created using either FILE3D or SKETCH3D you can. If you want to by pass creativity at this stage, alternate lines 60-130 are given after the program listing. These lines include data statements representing a 3D 'Wendy house' for you to draw on the screen.

PROJ3D program

```
10 REM ****PROGRAM PROJ3D****
20 REM DEMONSTRATES SIMPLE 3D PROJECTION METHOD
30 DIM X(50),Y(50),Z(50),LN(2,50)
40 DIM XP(50),YP(50)
45 CLS
50 REM GET DATA TO DRAW HOUSE
```

```
60 OPENIN "HOUSE.DAT"
70 INPUT£9,NPTS
80    FOR I=1 TO NPTS
90    INPUT£9,X(I),Y(I),Z(I)
100   XP(I)=X(I)
110   YP(I)=Y(I)
120   NEXT I
122   INPUT£9, LI
124   FOR I=1 TO LI
126    INPUT£9,LN(1,I),LN(2,I)
128   NEXT I
130 CLOSEIN
140 REM DRAW AXES
150 MOVE 180,280
160 DRAW 180,180
170 DRAW 280,180
180 REM NOW DRAW HOUSE
185 REM NOTE THAT COORDINATES ARE AT ORIGIN, WITH +200 TRANSLATION
190   FOR I=1 TO LI
200    MOVE XP(LN(1,I))+200,YP(LN(1,I))+200
210    DRAW XP(LN(2,I))+200,YP(LN(2,I))+200
220   NEXT I

230 END
```

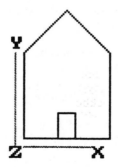

Figure 7.10 Output from PROJ3D showing front view of the Wendy house.

PROJ3D is a very simple program, and consists of the following sections

LINES 30- 40   SET UP ARRAYS
       60-130   INPUT DATA FOR HOUSE
      180-220   DRAW HOUSE

Lines 30-40

Although no transformations as such are to be done on the data in arrays X and

155

Y, arrays XP and YP are introduced, as they will be used extensively in later programs to hold transformed data.

Lines 60-130

The data read in is, as you would expect, identical to two dimensional data except for the addition of Z coordinates. The X and Y values are also stored in the XP and YP arrays as they are read in.

Lines 140-170

The X and Y axes are drawn to indicate the position of the displaced origin relative to the object. Again, this code is included only for compatibility with later programs.

Lines 180-220

Although the data is three dimensional, this simple projection does a 3D to 2D transformation by conveniently omitting the Z coordinate data altogether. Note the form of the **MOVE** and **DRAW** statements in lines 200-210. The coordinate data is drawn around the origin (ie, the 'invisible' centre point of the house is at 0,0. In order to translate the picture into the centre of the screen, a value of 200 is added to each X and Y coordinate value.

Here are the statements required to input the Wendy house data directly inside the program. Replace lines 50 - 130 with:

```
50    rem read in data for house
60    npts=14
70    for i=1 to 14:readx(i),y(i),z(i):xp=x(i):
      yp=y(i):next
80    lines=19
90    for i=1 to lines:readw(1,i),w(2,i):nexti
100   data0,0,0,0,45,0,22,60,0,45,45,0,45,0,0,0,
      0,40,0,45,40,22,60,40,45,45,40,45 40,45
110   data0,40,15,0,0,15,21,0,30,21,0,30,0,0,
      1,2,2,3,3,4,4,5,5,1,11,14,5,1,6,2,7
115   data3,8,4,9,5,10,6,7,7,8,8,9,9,10,10,6,11,
      12,12,13,13,14
```

Now whether you have drawn the Wendy house or have reconstructed your own data using FILE3D, you will not take long to notice that the effect of PROJ3D is to draw a single, very boring view of the object. No evidence of the object's 3D structure can be gained from the program as it stands. To 'pep it up', you need to transform the data.

7.5 Rotation, translation and scaling revisited

The real usefulness of 3D graphics is really only seen when the 3D data is made to work in some way, either by moving it around, or by using hidden line reconstruction methods. Of course, the particular techniques to be used depend on the application. Arcade type games programs or flight/driving simulators may need a lot of rotation and translation: the effect of flying a space ship around a three dimensional obstruction for example. Computer aided design programs may need an object to be displayed in as 'realistic' a manner as possible, and here the objects may need to show solid surfaces with hidden surface removal and shading.

As we did with the two dimensional case in Chapter 4, we'll take rotation first. As before, the donkey work will be done by matrix algebra, so if you want to know the nuts and bolts of the techniques involved, turn now to Appendix 2. In two dimensions, we merely had to specify the origin and we could rotate around this point. In three dimensions, we need to define a pivot axis. It is easiest to consider rotation around one of the coordinate axes X,Y or Z, so we will start by considering these 'axial' rotations. We will build up a three dimensional equivalent to TRV.. (described in Chapter 4), called TRANS3D. The code used for PROJ3D forms the basis for TRANS3D, and uses a rotation routine to set up the matrix for the 3D rotations.

TRANS3D program

```
10 REM ****PROGRAM TRANS3D****
20 REM DEMONSTRATES SIMPLE 3D PROJECTION METHOD
30 DIM X(30),Y(30),Z(30),LN(2,50),A(4,4)
40 DIM XP(30),YP(30)
50 CLS
55 MODE 1:INK 0,13:INK 1,1:INK 2,3
60 REM GET DATA TO DRAW HOUSE
70 OPENIN "HOUSE.DAT"
80 INPUT£9,NPTS
90    FOR I=1 TO NPTS
100      INPUT£9,X(I),Y(I),Z(I)
105 IF Z(I)>0 THEN Z(I)=Z(I)-60
110      XP(I)=X(I)
120      YP(I)=Y(I)
130      NEXT I
140      INPUT£9, LI
150      FOR I=1 TO LI
160        INPUT£9,LN(1,I),LN(2,I)
170      NEXT I
180 CLOSEIN
182 REM GET AXIS FOR ROTATION
```

```
183     INPUT"AXIS FOR ROTATION? - X=1,Y=2,Z=3";M
184     THETA=0
222     GOSUB 400:REM FULL ROTATION SETUP FIRST TIME ONLY
225 REM START MAIN LOOP FOR ROTATIONS
227 K$=INKEY$:IF K$="S"THEN CLS:GOTO 182:REM ABORT THIS ROTATION
230 REM NOW DRAW HOUSE
240 REM NOTE THAT COORDINATES ARE AT ORIGIN, WITH TRANSLATION TO CENTRE
245 CLS
247 GOSUB 1000:REM DRAW AXES
250     FOR I=1 TO LI
260         MOVE XP(LN(1,I))+320,YP(LN(1,I))+200
270         DRAW XP(LN(2,I))+320,YP(LN(2,I))+200,1,0
280     NEXT I
290 REM ROTATE THRU 10 DEGREES
300     THETA =THETA + 0.174533
310     A(M1,M2)=SIN(THETA)
311     A(M1,M1)=COS(THETA):A(M2,M2)=COS(THETA):A(M2,M1)=-SIN(THETA)
320 REM CALCULATE PROJECTION TO X,Y, PLANE
330     FOR I=1 TO NPTS
340         XP(I)=A(1,1)*X(I)+A(1,2)*Y(I)+A(1,3)*Z(I)+A(1,4)
350         YP(I)=A(2,1)*X(I)+A(2,2)*Y(I)+A(2,3)*Z(I)+A(2,4)
360     NEXT I
370 REM END OF MAIN LOOP
380 GOTO 225
400 REM SUBROUTINE ROTATE
410 C=COS(THETA)
420 S=SIN(THETA)
430     FOR K=1 TO 4
440     FOR L=1 TO 4
450         A(K,L)=0
460     NEXT L
470     NEXT K
475     REM NOW CALCULATE THE CORRECT INSERTIONS FOR THE MATRIX
476     REM SEE APPENDIX FOR THE THEORY!
480     A(4,4)=1
490     A(M,M)=1
500     M1=3-M:IF M1=0 THEN M1=1
510     M2=3:IF M=3 THEN M2=2
520     A(M1,M1)=C:A(M2,M2)=C:A(M2,M1)=-S:A(M1,M2)=S
530 RETURN
1000 REM DRAW AXES
1010     MOVE 310,300
1020     DRAW 310,190,2,0
1030     DRAW 400,190,2,0
1032     LOCATE 20,6:PRINT"Y"
1034     LOCATE 26,14:PRINT"X"
1036     LOCATE 20,14:PRINT"Z"
1040 RETURN
```

```
LINES
  30- 40   SET UP ARRAYS
  50- 55   SET UP COLOURS AND SCREEN
  60-180   INPUT DATA FOR HOUSE
 182-184   INPUT ROTATION AXIS,INITIALISE ROT ANGLE
 222       SETUP ROTATION MATRIX
 225       START MAIN LOOP
 200-220   DRAW HOUSE
 290-300   INCREMENT ANGLE, CALL ROTATION
           SUBROUTINE
 310-311   ADJUST ROTATION MATRIX
 320-360   CALCULATE PROJECTION TO X,Y, PLANE
 370       END OF MAIN LOOP
 400-530   SUBROUTINE ROTATE
1000-1040  DRAW AXES
```

Lines 10-247

This section of the program is largely the same as for PROJ3D except that the rotation axis M is chosen and the initial rotation angle is specified

Lines 290-311

The rotation angle is incremented. The trig functions in the rotation subroutine work in radians, so the incrementation is in 20 degree units (.174533*2 radians). As only a few of the rotation matrix values are changed for each angular increment these values are updated instead of updating the whole matrix each time.

Lines 320-360

The projection to the X,Y plane is performed using matrix algebra. The matrix multiplication here is the 4 x 4 rotation matrix held in array A, multiplied by the 4 x 1 vector holding X,Y and Z coordinates. The matrix multiplication works on the X,Y and Z arrays, but the results are put into the XP and YP arrays. This is to ensure that each multiplication is performed on the 'virgin' X,Y data to avoid 'rotating rotations'.

Lines 400-530

The rotate subroutine does not do any matrix multiplication, but merely fills the correct values into the rotation matrix A. The subroutine looks a little more complicated than it actually is because it uses the variable M to set which elements are filled with the various permutations of angles, 0's and 1's. Appendix 2 gives the form of the three rotation matrices around the major axes.

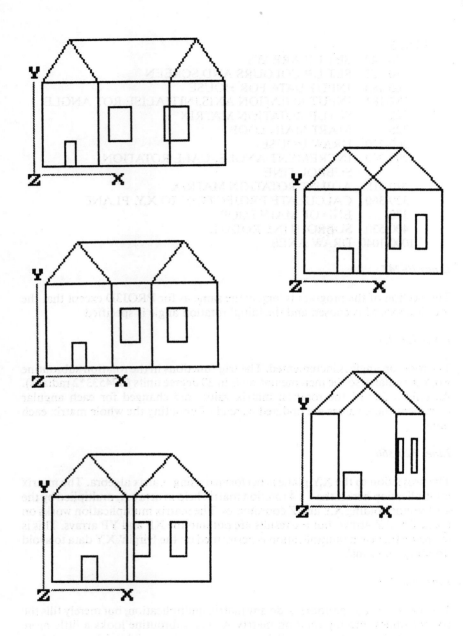

Figure 7.11 Output from TRANS3D showing rotation of the Wendy house around the Y axis.

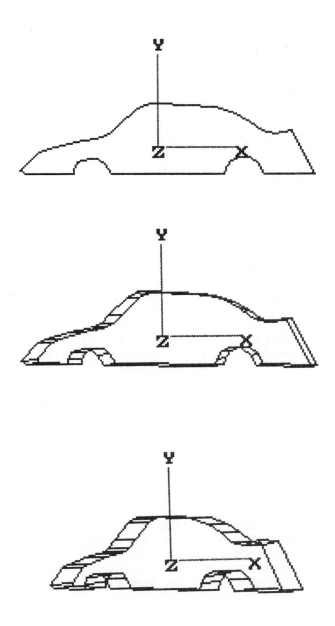

Figure 7.12 Output from TRANS3D showing rotation of a 'car chassis'. This shape was created using SKETCH3D as shown in Figure 7.8

If you run TRANS3D you will see the object rotating around one of the axes X,Y or Z. We have already seen that rotations are considerably easier if you stick to one of the major axes. Algorithms for more complex rotations can be found in the advanced graphics books listed in Appendix 3.

Scaling and translation both have equivalents to their two dimensional counterparts. The method for setting up and using the transformation matrices are also similar in two and three dimensions. The mathematical background to three dimensional transformations is given in Appendix 2, and the routines to add to TRANS3D are as follows:

```
1200 REM SUBROUTINE SCALE
1210 A(1,1)=SX:A(1,2)=0:A(1,3)=0:A(1,4)=0
1220 A(2,1)=0:A(2,2)=SY:A(2,3)=0:A(2,4)=0
1230 A(3,1)=0:A(3,2)=0:A(3,3)=SZ:A(3,4)=0
1240 A(4,1)=0:A(4,2)=0:A(4,3)=0:A(4,4)=1
1250 RETURN
1300 REM SUBROUTINE TRANSLATE
1310 A(1,1)=1:A(1,2)=0:A(1,3)=0:A(1,4)=TX
1320 A(2,1)=0:A(2,2)=1:A(2,3)=0:A(2,4)=TY
1330 A(3,1)=0:A(3,2)=0:A(3,3)=1:A(3,4)=TZ
1340 A(4,1)=0:A(4,2)=0:A(4,3)=0:A(4,4)=1
1350 RETURN
```

I will leave you the exercise of amending the programs in this chapter to make use of these routines.

7.6 Perspective projections

The algorithm that we will use for perspective projection is very simple, and is based on the following reasoning. Look at the next diagram. You can see that two sorts of projection plane are possible: those that are in front of the object and those that are behind the object. You can also see that the size of the image relative to the size of the object depends on the position of the perspective plane. If it is behind the object the projection is larger, but if it is in front of the object it is smaller. Note also that each point on the object maps to a corresponding point on the projection plane. The image is of course formed by drawing lines between the projected points as you would do with a two dimensional object (and this is why our W array is treated in the same way in 2 and 3D cases).

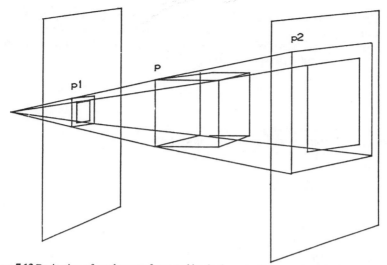

Figure 7.13 Projection of a cube onto front and back planes to show perspective. Face p is projected to p1 (front plane)and to p2 (rear plane).

The next diagram shows the geometrical relationship between the position of the point in 3D space and the position of the projection of the same point onto the screen. Let the projection plane be distance PP from the eye. For every point X, Y, Z, we must calculate the X,Y values at Z=PP. For the Y case, y/PP = Y/Z+PP, and y = Y*PP/Z+PP. in the same way, x = X*PP/Z+PP, so the calculations for the perspective view are now complete.

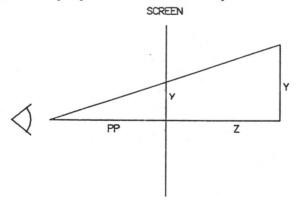

Figure 7.14 Relationship of the 'true' height of an object Y and its projection y onto the screen. As the distance from the observer to the screen (PP) and the Z value of the point, y can be calculated by similar triangles.

Now that the hard work has been done we can sit back and look at our perspective projections on the screen. As you will gather from the above description, we are not going to have to do much work in order to amend TRANS3D to handle perspective projections.

PER3D program

```
10 REM ****PROGRAM PER3D****
20 REM DEMONSTRATES PERSPECTIVE PROJECTION METHOD
30 DIM X(60),Y(60),Z(60),LN(2,80),A(4,4)
40 DIM XP(60),YP(60),ZP(60)
50 CLS
55 MODE 1:INK 0,13:INK 1,1:INK 2,3
60 INPUT"FILENAME";N$
70 OPENIN N$
80 INPUT£9,NPTS
90    FOR I=1 TO NPTS
100     INPUT£9,X(I),Y(I),Z(I)
105 IF Z(I)>0 THEN Z(I)=Z(I)-60
110     XP(I)=X(I)
120     YP(I)=Y(I)
125     ZP(I)=Z(I)
130     NEXT I
140     INPUT£9, LI
150     FOR I=1 TO LI
160       INPUT£9,LN(1,I),LN(2,I)
170     NEXT I
180 CLOSEIN
182 REM GET AXIS FOR ROTATION
183     INPUT"AXIS FOR ROTATION? - X=1,Y=2,Z=3";M
184     THETA=0
190 REM GET DISTANCE FROM OBSERVER TO ORIGIN
195     INPUT"DISTANCE FROM ORIGIN?";PP
222     GOSUB 400:REM FULL ROTATION SETUP FIRST TIME ONLY
225 REM START MAIN LOOP FOR ROTATIONS
227 K$=INKEY$:IF K$="S"THEN CLS:GOTO 182:REM ABORT THIS ROTATION
230 REM NOW DRAW HOUSE
240 REM NOTE THAT COORDINATES ARE AT ORIGIN, WITH TRANSLATION TO CENTRE
245 CLS
247 GOSUB 1000:REM DRAW AXES
250     FOR I=1 TO LI
260       MOVE XP(LN(1,I))+320,YP(LN(1,I))+200
270       DRAW XP(LN(2,I))+320,YP(LN(2,I))+200,1,0
280     NEXT I
290 REM ROTATE THRU 10 DEGREES
300     THETA =THETA + 0.174533
310     A(M1,M2)=SIN(THETA)
311     A(M1,M1)=COS(THETA):A(M2,M2)=COS(THETA):A(M2,M1)=-SIN(THETA)
312 REM NOW WIPE THE LAST PICTURE
313 GOTO 320
314     FOR I=1 TO LI
```

```
316        MOVE XP(LN(1,I))+200,YP(LN(1,I))+200
317        DRAW XP(LN(2,I))+200,YP(LN(2,I))+200,1,1
318     NEXT I
320 REM CALCULATE PROJECTION TO X,Y, PLANE
330     FOR I=1 TO NPTS
340        XT=A(1,1)*X(I)+A(1,2)*Y(I)+A(1,3)*Z(I)+A(1,4)
350        YT=A(2,1)*X(I)+A(2,2)*Y(I)+A(2,3)*Z(I)+A(2,4)
352        ZT=A(3,1)*X(I)+A(3,2)*Y(I)+A(3,3)*Z(I)+A(3,4)
354        DD=ZT+PP:XP(I)=XT*PP/DD:YP(I)=YT*PP/DD:ZP(I)=DD
360     NEXT I
370 REM END OF MAIN LOOP
380 GOTO 225
400 REM SUBROUTINE ROTATE
410 C=COS(THETA)
420 S=SIN(THETA)
430     FOR K=1 TO 4
440     FOR L=1 TO 4
450        A(K,L)=0
460     NEXT L
470     NEXT K
475     REM NOW CALCULATE THE CORRECT INSERTIONS FOR THE MATRIX
476     REM SEE APPENDIX FOR THE THEORY!
480     A(4,4)=1
490     A(M,M)=1
500     M1=3-M:IF M1=0 THEN M1=1
510     M2=3:IF M=3 THEN M2=2
520     A(M1,M1)=C:A(M2,M2)=C:A(M2,M1)=-S:A(M1,M2)=S
530 RETURN
1000 REM DRAW AXES
1010    MOVE 310,300
1020    DRAW 310,190,2,0
1030    DRAW 400,190,2,0
1032    LOCATE 20,6:PRINT"Y"
1034    LOCATE 26,14:PRINT"X"
1036    LOCATE 20,14:PRINT"Z"
1040 RETURN
```

LINES

310-311	ADJUST ROTATION MATRIX
320-360	CALCULATE PROJECTION TO X,Y PLANE
370	END MAIN LOOP FOR THIS ROTATION
400-520	ROTATE SUBROUTINE

Lines 60-180

The 3D data is read in as in the previous programs in this chapter.

Line 195

The variable PP is the distance from the eye to the origin, as described above.

Lines 320-360

The projection to the X,Y plane starts off with the calculation of values for the variables XT, YT, and ZT by matrix multiplication in a similar manner used to get the XP and YP values in TRANS3D. The data so far is a parallel projection, and the perspective transformation is done in line 260. In this line, the XP and YP (perspective) values are calculated by multiplying the parallel projections of XT and YT by the ratio of the distance from the observer to the origin (PP) over the distance from the observer to the Z coordinate of the point.

You can look at the effect of changing the position of the projection plane by changing the value of PP in the amended program. Clearly, the size of the picture will vary depending on the value of PP. If you consider the area of the projection plane to be the area of your monitor screen, then sensible values of PP would reflect the distance that you sit from the screen. The most 'realistic' distances are probably between PP = 2*h and PP = 3*h, where h is the height of the screen in pixels. So PP will normally be between 800 and 1200. But don't take my word for it! Experiment and see. If you make PP significantly larger than 600 you will get an almost parallel projection. If PP is less than 400, a distorted picture will result.

Now that we have looked at the complete armoury of three dimensional 'wire frame' techniques, you should experiment with various data sets and projections to gain familiarity with the various methods involved. It is important that you understand these basic techniques before going on to the next chapter, so that you can concentrate on the intricacies of hidden line methods.

One specialised form of '3D trickery' that you can perform is to make a *billboard*. In computer graphics jargon, a billboard is a 2D drawing or area of text displayed in 3D. This page of the book could be displayed on your TV or

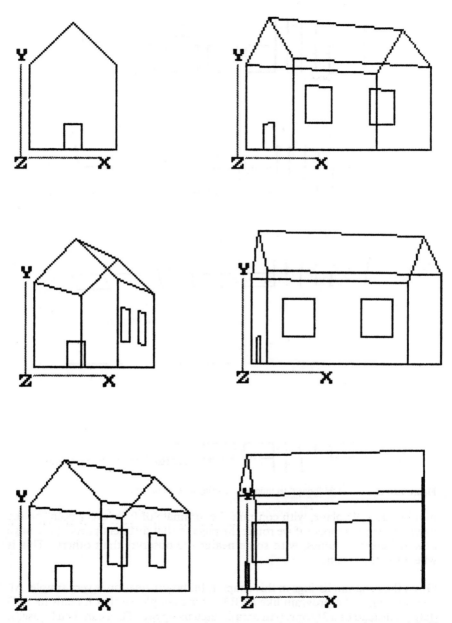

Figure 7.15 Output from PER3D showing the Wendy house rotation in perspective around the Y axis.

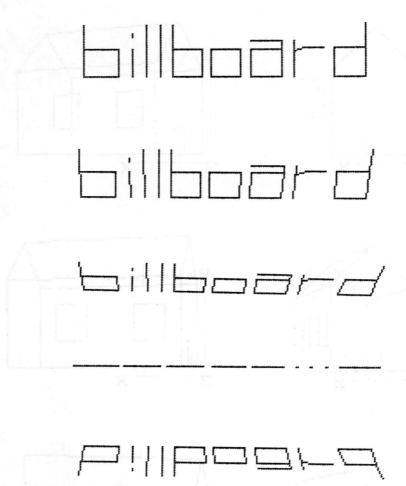

Figure 7.16 Use of the 'billboard' technique to display a 2D plane in 3D.

monitor as a 2D plane, with constant Z coordinate of 0 for every point on the page. But what happens if we rotate the page so that different parts of the page have different Z values, with some nearer the observer than others? This is where the fun begins.

Given the program listings in this chapter, billboard creation is very simple. All you do is amend a program like PER3D, for example, so that it reads in a 2D data set instead of a 3D one. (All data created using SKETCH can then be used). Next, you create an 'artificial' set of Z data to compensate for the missing data in the 2D data set. Try putting these alterations into PER3D.

```
10 REM **** BILLBOARD ****
12 REM ADDITIONS TO PER3D FOR 2D DATA INPUT
30 DIM X(500),Y(500),Z(500),LN(2,750),A(4,4)
40 DIM XP(500),YP(500),ZP(500)
100        INPUT£9,X(I),Y(I):Z(I)=0
```

It really is as simple as this!

Rotation of the picture will 'automatically' twist the billboard around X,Y or Z axes as required. Figures 7.16 and 7.17 show the technique in action. You will recognise the data set in Figure 7.17 as the USA map from Chapter 4. A 'satellite's eye view' has been created!

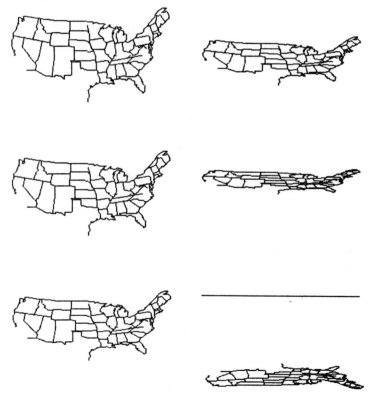

Figure 7.17 The data from Figure 4.9 were used to create this 'satellite view' of the USA.

Chapter 8

Hidden Lines and Surfaces

8.1 What is a hidden line?

The three dimensional objects that we considered in the last chapter were all of the 'wire frame' type. The Wendy house that we rotated in TRANS3D and PER3D appears confusing because it is often difficult to tell which is the front face and which is the rear. A method is therefore needed which 'cuts off' lines which should not be seen by the observer.

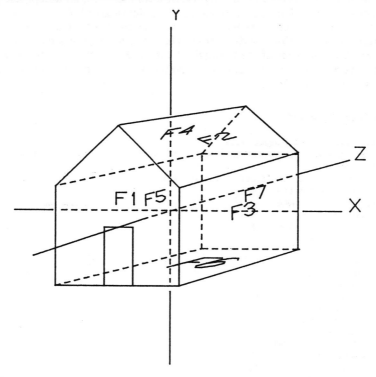

Figure 8.1 Outline of the Wendy house positioned around the origin. 'Hidden' lines are shown dotted. Each face is coded F1 - F7.

These cut off lines are called *hidden lines,* and many algorithms have been worked out to deal with them. Some methods are relatively simple, others are much more complex. The problem with all of these methods is the amount of processing time needed, especially when programming in BASIC. In this chapter we will look at one of the simplest types of hidden lines algorithms which can be used on Amstrad home computers.

Although it is quite usual to talk in terms of hidden lines, the term is not strictly accurate. We are not primarily interested in which *line* passes in front of another but rather which *surface.* We have not up until now considered surfaces at all, and so our first job in this chapter is to decide just what we mean by a surface, and how it can be described.

The simplest way of hiding lines and surfaces is to draw the surfaces starting with the surface furthest from the observer, working forwards to the 'front' of the screen. As long as certain criteria are met (the main one being that the surfaces are all drawn as solids by use of a fill method), an acceptable picture can be produced. This method is called a 'painters algorithm', as each successive surface 'paints' over underlying faces so that the new surface completely or partially obscures those underneath it. Here is a simple program that draws four rectangles. The order of the rectangles from back to front is black, blue, yellow and green, and the monochrome representation of the picture produced is shown in Figure 8.2

PAINTER program

```
10 REM **** PAINTER PROGRAM ****
20 REM DRAWS FOUR RECTANGLES TO DEMONSTRATE SIMPLE HIDDEN SURFACE METHOD
30 MODE 0
40 INK 0,13:INK 1,0:INK 2,2:INK 3,12:INK 4,9
50 REM DRAW RECTANGLES
60 REM BLACK RECTANGLE
70 GRAPHICS PEN 1
80    FOR Y=300 TO 200 STEP -1
90       MOVE 100,Y
100      DRAW 400,Y
110   NEXT Y
120 REM BLUE RECTANGLE
130 GRAPHICS PEN 2
140   FOR Y=350 TO 250 STEP -1
150      MOVE 150,Y
160      DRAW 350,Y
170   NEXT Y
180 REM YELLOW RECTANGLE
190 GRAPHICS PEN 3
200   FOR Y=250 TO 150 STEP -1
210      MOVE 200,Y
220      DRAW 400,Y
```

```
230    NEXT Y
240 REM GREEN RECTANGLE
250 GRAPHICS PEN 4
260    FOR Y=380 TO 200 STEP -1
270       MOVE 230,Y
280          DRAW 500,Y
290    NEXT Y
299 !COPY
300 STOP
```

Figure 8.2 Use of the 'painter's algorithm' to draw surfaces.

This method of overwriting colours is the same technique as we used for the
HISTO3D program in Chapter 5.

8.2 Defining surfaces

Let us review our structures for representing 3D data. We have arrays X, Y and
Z which hold sequential lists of the X, Y and Z coordinates for the points in the
picture. We also have an array W which contains the data for drawing lines

between the sets of coordinates. We now need to introduce two new arrays which will be used to hold the surface information. These arrays are called FA and NL. FA is dimensioned FA(i,j) where i is the number of lines defining surface j. The values in each element of the array are the indices held in our W array. Knowing the value of a given element of FA, then, allows us to access the coordinates of the points at either end of the line to which it refers. The second array, dimensioned NL(k), holds the number of lines defining each surface, with k representing the total number of surfaces.

If this is unclear, refer to the following diagram, which shows the relationship between all the arrays we have introduced so far: the data is for a cube. It is important that you take the trouble to work out this relationship, or else you will have difficulty in creating your own data sets for hidden lines treatment.

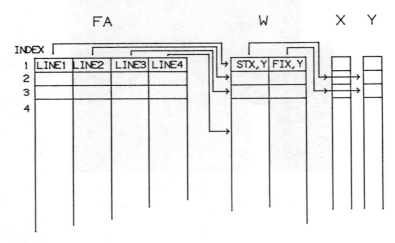

Figure 8.3 Relationship of FA, W, X and Y arrays (cf Figure 3.4). Here, each element for a particular index in FA 'points' to a line in the W array.

no.	X	Y	Z
1	− 50	− 50	− 50
2	− 50	50	− 50
3	50	50	− 50
4	50	− 50	− 50
5	− 50	− 50	50
6	− 50	50	50
7	50	50	50
8	50	− 50	50

no.	W 1	2
1	1	2
2	2	3
3	3	4
4	4	1
5	5	6
6	6	7
7	7	8
8	8	5
9	2	6
10	1	5
11	3	7
12	4	8

no.	NL	no.	FA 1	2	3	4
1	4	1	1	2	3	4
2	4	2	5	6	7	8
3	4	3	3	11	7	12
4	4	4	1	9	5	10
5	4	5	4	10	8	12
6	4	6	2	9	6	11

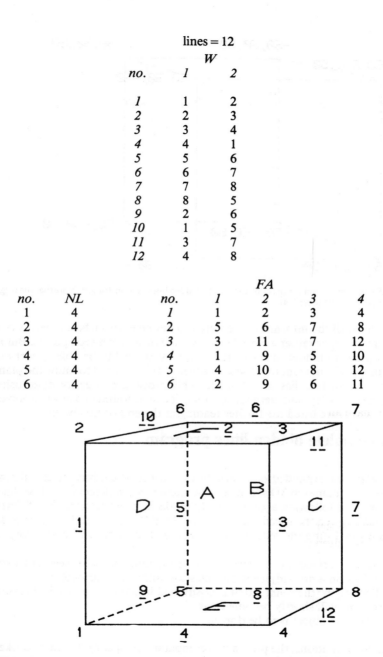

Figure 8.4 Point, line and face data for a cube. Lines are underlined here. The faces are labelled A - F.

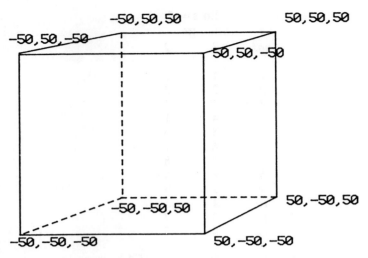

Figure 8.5 Coordinate data for the cube used in the hidden lines demonstration. Note that the origin is inside the cube (cf Figure 7.4).

We now have all the information required to define each surface in terms of a polygonal mesh, or rather a closed series of lines drawn between points. But in order to perform hidden surface analysis, we also need to be able to sort out which surfaces lie in front of others. In other words, we need to know the plane in which the surface lies in 3D space. This procedure is easily done using coordinate geometry, and methods for doing it can be found in many textbooks, some of which are listed for further reading at the end of this book.

8.3 A complete hidden lines program

Armed with our expanded data structures and the algorithm for calculating coefficients of planes in 3D space, we can attempt to implement a hidden lines algorithm. The following algorithm only works in a restricted range of cases. Nevertheless, given the speed limitations of BASIC it is a useful piece of code. Let us start by listing the restrictions on its use. The algorithm can be used if:

(1)   All the surfaces are convex (that is, every line drawn between any two points on a non-adjacent surface stays within the surface).
(2)   The origin (the point 0,0,0) is positioned inside the object. The reason for this will shortly become clear.
(3)   Only one object is to be drawn.

Given these limitations, the program is comparatively speedy. It can be broken down into the following steps.

176

(1)   Choose three points on each surface of the object.
(2)   Calculate the plane of the surface from the coordinates of the three points.
(3)   Check to see if the plane is between the origin and the observer.
(4)   Make a list of all the lines in all the planes which are between origin and observer.
(5)   Eliminate duplications in the list.
(6)   Draw the lines for a hidden lines picture.

All these elements are quite straightforward when looked at individually. The heaviest computation occurs in steps (4) and (5), because as each surface is processed and the line list is added to, redundancy occurs due to lines which are duplicated on several surfaces being repeated in the list. The redundant list entries are removed by (1) putting the list into a numeric order and then (2) stripping out duplications.

Satisfy yourself that all surfaces between you (the observer) and the origin are visible, and that all other surfaces are not visible in Figure 8.1

The data set used in HIDDEN may be created using FILE3DH, a version of FILE3D which allows the incorporation of the extra information needed to draw a hidden lines picture, namely the number of surfaces, number of lines around each surface and the codes of these lines so that they can be 'picked off' from the existing X, Y, Z and W arrays. Here is FILE3DH in full:

FILE3DH program

```
10 REM ****PROGRAM FILE3DH****
20 REM PROGRAM TO STORE COORDINATE DATA
25 REM VERSION FOR HIDDEN LINE REMOVAL
30    INPUT"FILENAME?";H$
40    OPENOUT H$
50    INPUT"NUMBER OF POINTS?";NPTS
55      WRITE£9,NPTS
60    PRINT"ENTER X,Y ,Z TRIPLETS"
70      FOR I=1 TO NPTS
80      INPUT"X, Y, Z=";X,Y,Z
90      WRITE£9,X
100     WRITE£9,Y
105 WRITE£9,Z
110     NEXT I
120     INPUT"NUMBER OF LINES?";LI
130     WRITE£9,LI
140     PRINT"ENTER NUMBERS OF JOINING POINTS"
150     FOR I=1 TO LI
160     INPUT"ST, FIN NOS=";SN,FI
170     WRITE£9,SN
```

```
180     WRITE£9,FI
190     NEXT I
200 REM NOW GET THE SURFACE DATA
210     INPUT"NUMBER OF SURFACES?";NF
215     PRINT£9,NF
220 REM DIMENSION SURFACE ARRAYS
230     DIM FA(12,NF),NL(NF)
240     PRINT"NOW INPUT CLOCKWISE LINES AROUND EACH SURFACE"
260     FOR I=1 TO NF
270        INPUT"NO OF LINES IN THIS SURFACE?";NLF
275           NL(I)=NLF
280           FOR J=1 TO NLF
290           INPUT "LINE=";LNUM
300           FA(J,I)=LNUM
310           PRINT£9,LNUM
320           NEXT J
330        REM NOW FILL ARRAY WITH ZEROS TO MAX LINE NO
340           IF NLF=12 THEN 390
350           FOR K=J TO 12
360           FA(K,I)=0
370           PRINT£9,0
380           NEXT K
390     NEXT I
400 REM NOW STORE LINES PER SURFACE ARRAY
410     FOR I=1 TO NF
420           PRINT£9,NL(I)
430     NEXT I
440 CLOSEOUT
450 END
```

The main hidden lines program HIDDEN is also reproduced in full here to save any confusion in adapting TRANS3D, on whose skeleton it is based. For your own convenience you will probably find it easier to load TRANS3D and to do extensive editing than to type the program from scratch.

HIDDEN program

```
5 REM ****PROGRAM HIDDEN****
10 REM USE PP=1000 TO TEST
20 MODE 1:INK 0,13:INK 1,1:INK 2,3
30 PP=1000
40 DIM X(40),Y(40),Z(40),LN(2,60),A(4,4),FA(12,40),NL(40),LS(40)
50 DIM XP(40),YP(40),ZP(40)
60 REM GET DATA TO DRAW SHAPE
70 INPUT"FILENAME?";H$:OPENIN H$
80     INPUT£9,NPTS
90     FOR I=1 TO NPTS
100     INPUT£9,X(I)
110       INPUT£9,Y(I)
120       INPUT£9,Z(I)
130       XP(I)=X(I):YP(I)=Y(I)
```

178

```
140     NEXT I
150   INPUT£9,LI
160   FOR I=1 TO LI
170     INPUT£9,LN(1,I),LN(2,I)
180   NEXT I
190   INPUT£9,NF
200   FOR I=1 TO NF
210     FOR J=1 TO 12
220       INPUT£9,FA(J,I)
230     NEXT J
240   NEXT I
250   FOR I=1 TO NF
260     INPUT£9,NL(I)
270   NEXT I
280   CLOSEIN
290   REM GET AXIS FOR ROTATION
300 REM GET AXIS FOR ROTATION
310   INPUT"AXIS FOR ROTATION? - X=1,Y=2,Z=3";M
320   THETA=0
330   GOSUB 540:REM FULL ROTATION SETUP FIRST TIME ONLY
340 REM START MAIN LOOP FOR ROTATIONS
350 K$=INKEY$:IF K$="S"THEN CLS:GOTO 300:REM ABORT THIS ROTATION
360 REM NOW DRAW OBJECT
370 REM NOTE THAT COORDINATES ARE AT ORIGIN, WITH TRANSLATION TO CENTRE
380 CLS
390 GOSUB 700:REM DRAW AXES
400 REM ROTATE THRU 10 DEGREES
410   THETA =THETA + 0.174533
420   A(M1,M2)=SIN(THETA)
430   A(M1,M1)=COS(THETA):A(M2,M2)=COS(THETA):A(M2,M1)=-SIN(THETA)
440 REM CALCULATE PROJECTION TO X,Y, PLANE
450   FOR I=1 TO NPTS
460     XT=A(1,1)*X(I)+A(1,2)*Y(I)+A(1,3)*Z(I)+A(1,4)
470     YT=A(2,1)*X(I)+A(2,2)*Y(I)+A(2,3)*Z(I)+A(2,4)
480     ZT=A(3,1)*X(I)+A(3,2)*Y(I)+A(3,3)*Z(I)+A(3,4)
490     DD=ZT+PP:XP(I)=XT*PP/DD:YP(I)=YT*PP/DD:ZP(I)=ZT
500   NEXT I
510 GOSUB 780:REM HIDDEN LINES ROUTINE
520 REM END OF MAIN LOOP
530 GOTO 340
540 REM SUBROUTINE ROTATE
550 C=COS(THETA)
560 S=SIN(THETA)
570   FOR K=1 TO 4
580   FOR L=1 TO 4
590     A(K,L)=0
600   NEXT L
610   NEXT K
620   REM NOW CALCULATE THE CORRECT INSERTIONS FOR THE MATRIX
630   REM SEE APPENDIX FOR THE THEORY!
640   A(4,4)=1
650   A(M,M)=1
660   M1=3-M:IF M1=0 THEN M1=1
670   M2=3:IF M=3 THEN M2=2
```

179

```
680     A(M1,M1)=C:A(M2,M2)=C:A(M2,M1)=-S:A(M1,M2)=S
690 RETURN
700 REM DRAW AXES
710     MOVE 310,300
720     DRAW 310,190,2,0
730     DRAW 400,190,2,0
740     LOCATE 20,6:PRINT"Y"
750     LOCATE 26,14:PRINT"X"
760     LOCATE 20,14:PRINT"Z"
770 RETURN
780 REM SUBROUTINE HIDDEN
790     IC=0:C=0:REM SETUP COUNTERS
800 REM GET POINTS IN THE PLANE
810     FOR IH=1 TO NF
820       I1=FA(1,IH):I2=FA(2,IH)
830       I5=LN(1,I1):I6=LN(2,I1):I7=LN(1,I2)
840       IF (I5=I7) OR (I6=I7) THEN I7=LN(2,I2)
850 REM NOW CALCULATE PLANE POSITION
860     X5=XP(I5)-XP(I6):Y5=YP(I5)-YP(I6):Z5=ZP(I5)-ZP(I6)
870     X6=XP(I7)-XP(I6):Y6=YP(I7)-YP(I6):Z6=ZP(I7)-ZP(I6)
880       A9=Y5*Z6-Y6*Z5
890       B9=Z5*X6-Z6*X5
900       C9=X5*Y6-X6*Y5
910       D9=A9*XP(I5)+B9*YP(I5)+C9*ZP(I5)
920 REM ARE OBSERVER AND ORIGIN ON DIFFERENT SIDES OF THE PLANE?
925     IF D9=0 THEN F9=0:GOTO 940:REM AVOID DIVIDE BY ZERO
930     F9=(1+C9*PP)/D9
940     IF F9>=0 THEN 1010
950 C=C+1
960 IX=NL(IH)
970     FOR JH=1 TO IX
980       IC=IC+1
990       LS(IC)=FA(JH,IH)
1000    NEXT JH
1010    NEXT IH
1020 REM ORDER THE LIST
1030    FOR IH=1 TO IC-1
1040      II=IH+1
1050      LL=LS(IH)
1060    FOR JH=II TO IC
1070      IF LL<=LS(JH) THEN 1110
1080      LL=LS(JH)
1090      LS(JH)=LS(IH)
1100      LS(IH)=LL
1110    NEXT JH
1120    NEXT IH
1130 REM NOW GET RID OF DUPLICATIONS IN THE LIST
1140      JH=1
1150      FOR IH=2 TO IC
1160      IF LS(IH)=LS(JH) THEN 1190
1170        JH=JH+1
1180        LS(JH)=LS(IH)
1190      NEXT IH
1200      IC=JH
```

```
1210    IN=1
1220    LQ=LS(1)
1230 REM NOW DRAW THE PICTURE USING LINES IN LIST ONLY
1240    FOR IH=1 TO LI
1250      L2=LN(2,IH)
1260      L1=LN(1,IH)
1270    IF IH<>LQ OR IN>IC THEN 1320
1280      MOVE XP(L1)+320,YP(L1)+200
1290      DRAW XP(L2)+320,YP(L2)+200,1,0
1300      IN=IN+1
1310      LQ=LS(IN)
1320    NEXT IH
1330 FOR I=1 TO 1000:NEXT I
1340 RETURN
```

HIDDEN consists of the following sections

Lines 10-770

All the steps here are identical to those met in the last chapter in the program PER3D. This part of the program draws and rotates a cube in perspective around one of the major axes. The section for inputting the object data (lines 70-280) is expanded to read the surface data into the arrays FA and NL. The axis draw section (subroutine at lines 700-770) is only for demonstration purposes and can be omitted as required.

Line 790

The two counters IC and C are initialised. C is the number of surfaces to be displayed after hidden line removal. IC is the number of lines in the LS list.

Lines 800-840

The method for finding which surfaces are visible depends on calculation of a 'plane coefficient' for each face. This plane coefficient is found from the positions of three points on each face. The first two lines in each face are obtained from the FA array (and are placed in variables I1 and I2).

The points at the start of the first line and the start of the second line are then obtained from the W array, and are in turn placed in variables I5 and I6. The point at the end of the first line is placed in variable I7. If either I5 or I6 = I7 then the end point of the second line is placed in I7.

Lines 850-910

The plane position is calculated in the following manner. The difference between the X and Y and Z coordinates of the points I5 and I6, and I6 and I7 are placed in variables X5, Y5, Z5 and X6, Y6, and Z6.

Variables A9, B9, and C9 are then calculated, and variable D9 is found from these values. The plane coefficient F9 is then calculated in line 640. If this coefficient is less than or equal to 0.0, it means that the surface is not between the observer and the origin, so the surface is discarded.

Lines 950-1000

All the lines in the surface (if it has not been discarded) must now be stored in an array which will be used to draw the final picture. Counter C is incremented (one more surface), and the variable IX is set to the number of lines in the surface (using the NL array for reference: note that the loop variable IH will be set at the correct surface number). The counter IC is incremented for each new line, and the FA array is used to obtain each successive line for the surface being processed. These lines are then put into the LS array. Note also that the line indices held in LS are not segregated specifically into surfaces, LS merely holds a list of lines.

Lines 1020-1190

The next stage is carried out when all surfaces have been processed, and involves first ordering the LS array, so that all line 'repeats' (ie occurrences of the same line in two visible faces) are grouped. After this ordering has been carried out (lines 1020-1120) it is easier to remove all multiple occurrences of the same line (lines 1130-1190). I leave you to work out how these two steps are performed!

Lines 1200-1220

IC is no longer a true indicator of the number of lines because of the removal of duplications. You can see from line 840 than JH is used temporarily to store the 'reduced' number of lines. IC must therefore be reset to JH. Variable LQ is used to hold the current line number (from the LS list), and IN is a counter for the LS list.

Lines 1230-1320

The picture is drawn in essentially the same manner as was used for PER3D in the last chapter. The main difference is that LQ is only changed once the current 'visible' line has been reached in the main line list. If the line currently being processed is LQ then it is drawn, IN is incremented, and LQ is assigned the value of the next LS element. In other words, LQ becomes the next line number which may be drawn.

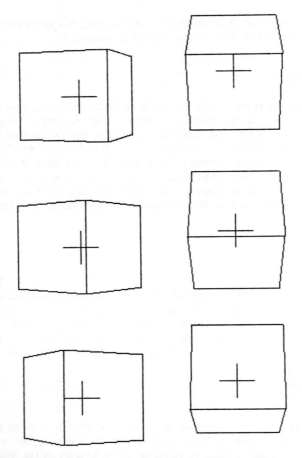

Figure 8.6 Output from HIDDEN showing cube rotation around the X and Y axes.

You can use HIDDEN for any 3D data set which is not concave, so long as the origin is set inside it. This of course just means that coordinate 0,0,0 must be inside the figure. But you shouldn't think that this limitation restricts you to viewing the picture in the bottom left hand corner of the screen! It does mean that you must use the scaling and translating routines after hidden lines processing to position the drawing where you want it on the screen. There is in fact a short cut to this repositioning process, and this short cut has been used in HIDDEN. All I've done is to add + 30 to the final X and Y coordinates at the time of plotting. This increment is completely arbitrary and could be anything between 0-639 X and 0-399 Y depending on the original position of the picture to be transformed.

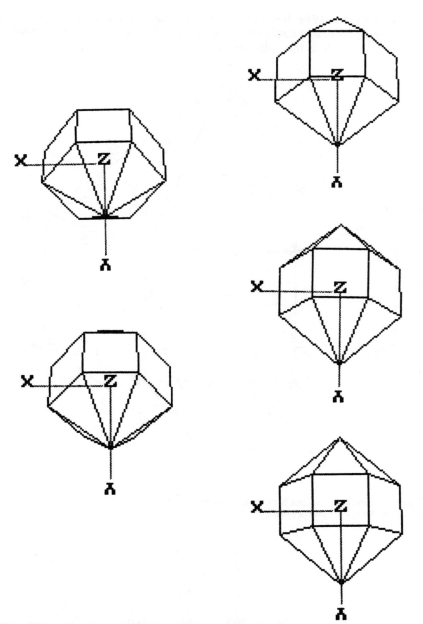

Figure 8.7 Output from HIDDEN showing hidden lines picture of a 'crystal'. Rotations are around the X, Y and Z axes, (left, centre and right columns respectively).

The figure above may be drawn using the following data set. Although the shape is more complex than a straightforward cube, it still fulfills the criteria needed for our simple hidden lines algorithm to work.

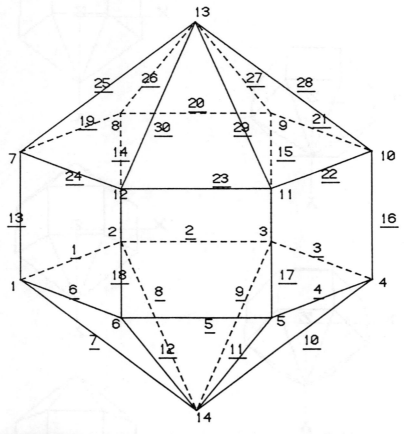

Figure 8.8 Point and line data for a 14-gon 'crystal'. The surface data has been omitted from this figure for clarity (see data below).

| no. | npts = 14 | | |
	X	Y	Z
1	100	70	0
2	140	70	-60
3	200	70	-60
4	240	70	0

5	200	70	60
6	140	70	60
7	100	130	0
8	140	130	− 60
9	200	130	− 60
10	240	130	0
11	200	130	60
12	140	130	60
13	170	190	0
14	170	10	0

lines = 30

	W			W	
no.	1	2	*no.*	1	2
1	1	2	*15*	3	9
2	2	3	*16*	4	10
3	3	4	*17*	5	11
4	4	5	*18*	6	12
5	5	6	*19*	7	8
6	6	1	*20*	8	9
7	1	14	*21*	9	10
8	2	14	*22*	10	11
9	3	14	*23*	11	12
10	4	14	*24*	12	7
11	5	14	*25*	7	13
12	6	14	*26*	8	13
13	1	7	*27*	9	13
14	2	8	*28*	10	13
			29	11	13
			30	12	13

		FA			
no.	*NL*	*1*	*2*	*3*	*4*
1	4	13	1	14	19
2	4	14	2	15	20
3	4	15	3	16	21
4	4	16	4	17	22
5	4	17	5	18	23
6	4	18	6	13	24
7	3	19	26	25	0
8	3	20	27	26	0
9	3	21	28	27	0
10	3	22	29	28	0

11	3	23	30	29	0
12	3	24	25	30	0
13	3	1	7	8	0
14	3	2	8	9	0
15	3	3	9	10	0
16	3	4	10	11	0
17	3	5	11	12	0
18	3	6	12	7	0

8.4 Extension of SKETCH3D

The extension of SKETCH which allows 3D data sets to be composed on screen can itself be extended to include surface data. The extra lines to add to SKETCH3D are given below, and we will call this new version SKETCH3DH. The surface data is made up of the initial outline (surface one), the duplicate outline (surface two), together with the other surfaces, each of which is a rectangle, made up of each line on surface one, its duplicate on surface two, and the lines which join the points at either end of the first two lines on the two surfaces. These surfaces are indicated in the following figure.

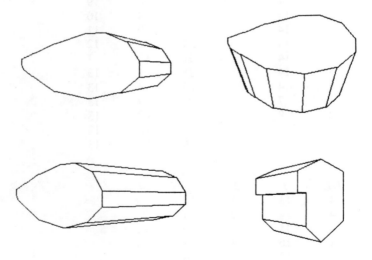

Figure 8.9 Output from SKETCH3DH. The picture at the bottom right shows that even a non convex shape can be drawn with the HIDDEN program in a few cases.

The main HIDDEN program needs several alterations to work well with SKETCH3DH. These alterations mainly consist of calculation of the centre point of the data, with translation of this point to the origin. All other points are translated by the same negative displacement. You will recall that we used this technique to transform the segment data in the DESIGN program (Chapter 6). Only X and Y points need to be transformed, because SKETCH3DH automatically sets the Z values of the front and rear surfaces to be greater than and less than 0 respectively. Here are the changes that need to be made to SKETCH3D.

SKETCH3DH program

```
10 REM **** PROGRAM SKETCH3DH ****
110 S(1,2)=0
800 REM NOW CREATE FILE CONTAINING DATA
810 OPENOUT N$
815 GOSUb 1200:REM GET TRANSLATION VALUES
817 PRINT "YOUR X SPREAD IS ",XH-XL
818 PRINT "YOUR Y SPREAD IS ",YH-YL
819 INPUT "INPUT YOUR Z SPREAD";ZZ
820     PRINT£9,NA*2
830     FOR I=1 TO NA
840        PRINT£9,XP(I)+XTRANS
850        PRINT£9,YP(I)+YTRANS
860        PRINT£9,-(ZZ/2)
870     NEXT I
875 REM OVERWRITE THIS LINE
880     FOR I=1 TO NA
890        PRINT£9,XP(I)+XTRANS
900        PRINT£9,YP(I)+YTRANS
910        PRINT£9,(ZZ/2)
915 REM OVERWRITE THIS LINE
920     NEXT I
930 REM IF S(1,2)=0 THEN S(1,2)=LB
940     PRINT£9,(3*LB)+1
950     FOR I=1 TO LB
960        PRINT£9,LN(1,I),LN(2,I)
965 REM OVERWRITE THIS LINE
970     NEXT I
980     FOR I=1 TO LB
990        PRINT£9,LN(1,I)+NA
1000       PRINT£9,LN(2,I)+NA
1010    NEXT I
1020    FOR I=1 TO LB
1030       PRINT£9,I
1040       PRINT£9,I+NA
1050    NEXT I
1060    PRINT£9,LB+1
1070    PRINT£9,LB+1+NA
1080    PRINT£9,LB+2
1090     FOR I=1 TO LB
1100        PRINT£9,I
```

```
1110    NEXT I
1120      FOR I=1 TO LB
1130        PRINT£9,I+LB
1140      NEXT I
1150      FOR I=1 TO LB+1
1160        PRINT£9,I,I+(2*LB),I+LB,I+(2*LB)+1
1170      NEXT I
1180      PRINT£9,LB:PRINT£9,LB
1185      FOR I=1 TO LB
1190        PRINT£9,4
1192      NEXT I
1194 CLOSEOUT
1196 END
1200 REM ROUTINE TO TRANSLATE X,Y VALS AROUND ORIGIN
1205 XL=640:YL=400:XH=0:YH=0
1210      FOR I=1 TO NA
1220        IF XP(I)<XL THEN XL=XP(I)
1230        IF XP(I)>XH THEN XH=XP(I)
1240        IF YP(I)<YL THEN YL=YP(I)
1250        IF YP(I)>YH THEN YH=YP(I)
1260      NEXT I
1270 XTRANS = -((XH+XL)/2)
1280 YTRANS = -((YH+YL)/2)
1290 RETURN
```

These changes may appear a bit complex, so you may find the following notes of help.

Line 815, subroutine at line 1200

The picture created using SKETCH3D will be placed at some arbitrary point on the screen, and will not be centred around the origin. The first job of the amended program is therefore to work out the translation necessary to move all the data points to new locations around the origin (we have already used this technique in the DESIGN program in chapter 6).

Lines 1200-1260

The minimum and maximum X and Y coordinates for the data set are calculated.

Lines 1270-1280

The X and Y translation variables XTRANS and YTRANS are calculated in these lines.

Lines 1020-1192

This new section handles the surface data. As you will appreciate, the front and back surfaces of any object created using SKETCH3DH will have a variable number of sides, whilst all the other surfaces have four sides, one each at front and back, and two joining front and back surfaces. Line XXX inputs the total number of lines, and works out LT, the number of lines on each of the front and back surfaces from this.

In line 142 the number of surfaces is inputted, and the arrays FA and NL are dimensioned using this information. Lines 144-148 contain the surface data input statements, and line 150 sets the number of lines within each surface.

To use SKETCH3DH you will also need to make some amendments to the HIDDEN program. Here are the alterations. As before, MERGE these lines with HIDDEN already in memory.

```
10 REM **** HIDDEN2 - FOR USE WITH S3DH ****
200     LT=(LI-1)/3
205     FOR I=1 TO LT
210         INPUT£9,FA(I,1)
215     NEXT I
220     FOR I=1 TO LT
225         INPUT£9,FA(I,2)
230     NEXT I
235     FOR I=3 TO NF
240         INPUT£9,FA(1,I),FA(2,I),FA(3,I),FA(4,I)
245     NEXT I
250     NL(1)=LT:NL(2)=LT
255     FOR I=3 TO NF
260         NL(I)=4
270     NEXT I
```

8.5 More advanced techniques

HIDDEN will not work properly on pictures with more than one object (the origin cannot be inside two objects at once, unless they surround each other). This is perhaps the biggest disadvantage of what is a relatively simple and speedy algorithm. If you wish to use a more ambitious hidden surface approach, then it is not really feasible to use an Amstrad BASIC program because of the time it will take to process the picture. If you do want to delve further into the world of advanced computer graphics, some books are listed in Appendix 3. You may find some of these texts heavy going, but you have a sufficient grounding in graphics techniques now to tackle some demanding homework! During the preparation of this book I toyed with the idea of including a more sophisticated hidden lines algorithm (a BASIC version of the algorithm given in Angell's book referenced in Appendix 3). My poor Amstrad took five minutes to plot a 20 point hidden lines picture using this algorithm, so I reluctantly decided not to include the details here.

There are in fact many hidden surface algorithms, and one in particular is worthy of further mention here because it is so conceptually simple, yet tantalisingly difficult to implement on a low memory computer. This is the *depth-buffer* algorithm. In depth buffering, each pixel is assigned depth information. The visible screen of the monitor is viewed as a long narrow box measuring the standard X by Y pixels, but with depth, or the Z dimension extending back into the screen. Associated with the main bit map, there is an additional memory area which contains the Z value for each pixel.

To start with, the Z value of all pixels is set to the maximum value. The depth memory then has the equivalent of a solid surface across the furthest end of the box. Next, a surface is written into the bit map. Each pixel that makes up the polygon depth is compared with the value already in the depth buffer for that location. If the new value of a pixel is less than its existing value, it is itself written into the bit map, and its Z value is substituted for the old value in the depth buffer. Because all locations of the buffer have been preset to the maximum value, all the pixels of the first surface are written. Z values for pixels that are not on the lines defining the surface are found by mathematical means, in a similar way to that used in filling a shape.

If, on drawing a subsequent surface the new Z value is further away than the Z value already existing for a particular pixel, it should be hidden and not drawn. If on the other hand the Z value is less than the existing pixel, it is closer to the screen, and should overwrite the existing point. The effect of repeating this procedure for all points is that only the visible surfaces are drawn. Note that the surfaces need not be processed in any particular order. The main overhead in this hidden surface method is the size of the Z buffer. It would be difficult to operate with less than two bytes per pixel: even the Amstrad's memory does not have 128K bytes spare!

Nevertheless, this technique presents possibilities for the enterprising machine code programmer. A 'Z buffer extension ROM' could be developed for the Amstrad machines which would enable very sophisticated real time hidden lines programming. Is this just a dream? Modern graphics systems coupled to mini and mainframe computers have depth buffering and can shade a 640 X 512 pixel picture with up to 5000 surfaces in from two to five seconds. The cost? Around £20,000 - £30,000 at 1985 prices.

Chapter Nine

A Sample Application: Drawing Molecules

9.1 Setting the scene

In all the earlier chapters of this book we have looked in quite general terms at the sorts of graphics approaches and techniques that you can use on your Amstrad. In this final chapter we will consider a rather more specialised case history: how to draw atoms and molecules on a home computer. At this point I must reveal a little of my own background. My main training has been as a biologist and although my interest in computers submerges this other interest from time to time there are quite a few occasions when the two fields work together very well. Graphics are used in various biological disciplines, from the use of graphs and histograms in the plotting of experimental data to the use of complex graphics simulation techniques. One of the most colourful uses of graphics in the life sciences is the reconstruction of the appearance of biological molecules from spatial coordinate data of the constituent atoms.

As you are probably aware, all matter is made up of atoms arranged in characteristic groups called molecules, and the proportions and types of different atoms in substances can be gauged by the technique of X-ray crystallograpy. Many different methods for reconstructing the appearance of molecules have been devised, from crude representation made out of 'coat-hanger wire' to specially designed plastic kits. Most recently, computer graphics reconstructions have been used, and you may have seen examples of the impressive pictures produced by the most expensive graphics systems. Our problem is therefore this. Can we use an Amstrad computer to draw pictures of molecules from a set of coordinate data?

9.2 Solving the problem

The most important question to ask is, therefore, what elements of a computer system are necessary to draw molecules? The answer is not clear-cut. As with any computer work there are trade-offs to consider. Let us start with the essentials. What do we need in a graphics system to do this kind of work? Firstly, the system must be able to display non-text graphics. Next, there must be sufficient processing power and memory available to calculate coordinate positions in three dimensional space and to do the relevent 3-space to 2-space projections that we have already seen in Chapter 7. So far so good. But what about the actual appearance of the atoms within a molecule? Should all the atomic particles be drawn? Should a hidden lines algorithm be used? What about colour and definition?

Few molecular models consider atomic particles at all. This is for reasons of clarity rather than any inherent difficulty in drawing the particles. Molecules are of interest to biologists primarily because of their arrangements of atoms, not because of the arrangements of the subatomic particles. Molecules are characteristically modelled on computers as opaque or transparent spheres, with the outer electron orbit (ie the maximum physical diameter of an atom) as the diameter of the sphere. In 'ball' models, only the atom positions are modelled. An alternative method of display is to join atoms that are chemically joined in each molecule (the so-called 'ball and stick' model). The form of the balls is also open to a variety of display treatments. Is a 'true' spherical representation to be used, or will a common or garden circle do? Is the sphere to show shading,incident and reflected light?

We can now begin to narrow down our Amstrad options. To start with, phenomena like light reflection and true shading are both computationally very intense and need a huge palette of colours (say of the order of 64 grey shades for an absolute minimum representation in monochrome only). Light ray tracing also needs a very high resolution graphics system, say 1024 X 1024 pixel resolution. At the time of writing, the display device alone (forget the computer) would not leave much change from £10,000. We will therefore stick with 'common or garden circles'.

But this is where the fun begins. What we are really trying to do is to play the 'big boys' game with our humble home computer. What tricks can we use to make up for the lack of mainframe processing power and resolution on the Amstrad machines? Trick number one relies on the human eye. If a smooth non-reflectant sphere is observed under even lighting conditions at a distance it is impossible to distinguish it from a two dimensional coloured circle. This means that our simple Amstrad circles can perform a good simulation of a sphere!

If you have read Chapter 7 (and I hope that by now you have read it), you will recall that transforming points in three dimensional space is really not too difficult. If you think of a set of data for drawing a molecule as a set of X,Y,Z points for the centre of each atom in the molecule, together with the type of each atom (used to set its diameter), then the glimmerings of the structure of a primitive program for molecule drawing appears. The form could be as follows:

(1)   Read in the X,Y,Z and type data for each atom.

(2)   Do a 3-space to 2-space projection for the data points.

(3)   Scale the data to fit a 640 X 400 coordinate space.

(4)   Draw a circle of the correct diameter around the projected centre
point of each atom, using a different colour for each atom type.

Our molecule drawing program has been born!

9.3 Developing the program

As you are probably aware by now, writing a computer program takes ten times
as long as you initially thought it would. The more complex the program, the
more time you waste trying endless variations and debugging seemingly perfect
pieces of code that just do not work. Let us give the Amstrad molecule drawing
program a name - MOL3D. MOL3D is a typical product of a number of
sleepless nights - it was originally supposed to be written in an evening's session!

The simple program that was outlined at the end of the last section is in fact very
straightforward. The problem is that the picture produced is very confusing
(Figure 9.1). No illusion of depth is given and the whole thing is really a mess.
We need to colour the 'spheres' using a fill algorithm and we also need to use a
hidden surface method so that spheres further from the observer are hidden
behind those closer up as shown in Figure 9.2. How do we do this?

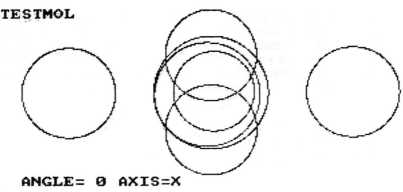

TESTMOL

ANGLE= 0 AXIS=X

Figure 9.1 The open circle method for drawing molecules.

TESTMOL

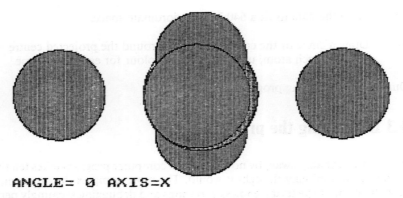

ANGLE= 0 AXIS=X

Figure 9.2 Filled circle view of the molecule shown in Figure 9.1

The secret is to use a sorting algorithm to sort all the atoms in the molecule by means of their Z coordiinates. We then end up with a list of atoms with atom number one closest to the observer and the last atom furthest away from the observer. We can then use a 'painter's algorithm' as discussed at the beginning of the last chapter to give a simple method of hidden surface elimination.. Here is the section of MOL3D that does the sorting.

```
3000 REM SUBROUTINE FOR SORT
3010   FOR K=1 TO NPTS
3020   FOR J=1 TO NPTS
3030     ZZ=ZP(K)
3040     YY=YP(K)
3050     XX=XP(K)
3060     SN=SS(K):REM STORE TEMPORARY VALUES
3065     SM=SI(K)
3070     IF ZP(J)<=ZP(K) THEN 3110
3080     ZP(K)=ZP(J):ZP(J)=ZZ
3090     YP(K)=YP(J):YP(J)=YY
3100     XP(K)=XP(J):XP(J)=XX
3105     SS(K)=SS(J):SS(J)=SN
3107     SI(K)=SI(J):SI(J)=SM
3110   NEXT J
3120   NEXT K
3130 RETURN
```

There are however two problems with the basic painter's algorithm approach in this case. If you have a CPC464 you have no fill command to paint in the circles, but here is your salvation. Replace the references to FILL in MOL3D with GOSUB 6000 and add the following lines to the complete program.

```
100 CLG
500 INK 2,3
510 INK 1,1
6000 REM CIRCLE FILL FOR CPC464 ONLY
6005 PD=2:REM SET DRAW COLOUR
6010 AN=0.017455*2
6015 R=50
6020 AI=0:AJ=0
6030 XL=320:YL=200
6040    FOR II=1 TO 200
6050       AI=AI+AN
6060       AJ=AI-(2*PI)
6070       AX=XL+(R*COS(AI))
6080       AY=YL+(R*SIN(AI))
6090       BX=XL-(R*COS(AJ))
6095       BY=YL+(R*SIN(AJ))
6100          FOR JJ=BX TO AX
6110             IF TEST( JJ,AY)=0 THEN PLOT JJ,AY,PD
6120          NEXT JJ
6130    NEXT II
```

There is still another problem. It is fine to draw all the spheres in the same colour but to FILL them in the colour-coded scheme for the correct types of atoms is difficult. If you try to use the CPC 6128/664 FILL command to do this you are in for a shock. The FILL operation stops when it reaches a boundary of the current drawing ink colour. The painter's algorithm will not therefore erase the boundary lines around more distant atoms as it draws them.

My own solution was to turn the painter's algorithm on its head and to draw the atoms nearest first. Instead of overwriting all closer atoms, each pixel on the boundaries of further atoms is tested before being drawn to see if a closer atom is being overwritten. If it is, the drawing operation on that part of the atom is halted. This method gives a perfect hidden surface view, as you can see from Figure 9.2

If every pixel around the boundary of every atom is to be plotted, a significant amount of time will be spent plotting circles. We have already looked at a circle drawing algorithm in Chapter 1, but time was not a major consideration at that point. Can we in fact speed up circle drawing? Luckily help is at hand, in the guise of a technique called eight-way symmetry (Figure 9.3). This technique relies on the fact that the points in all eight octants of a circle can be quickly found from the coordinates of the points in the first octant. The code is given in the routine at line 3500 of MOL3D. The circle generation algorithm (line 2160-2240) therefore only needs to calculate the first 45 degrees of each circle, relying on eight-way symmetry to fill in the remaining quadrants.

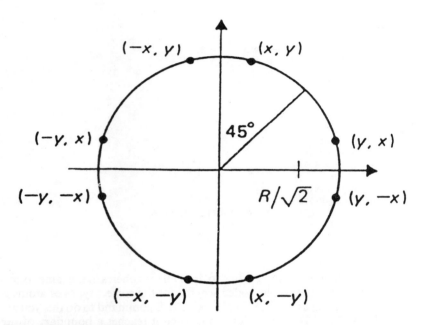

Figure 9.3 The eight symmetrical points on a circle.

Our program is now in essence complete. The other elements (projection, scaling, data input) are similar to those discussed in Chapter 7.

9.4 The full MOL3D program

MOL3D program

```
10 REM **** MOL3D - 3D MOLECULE PROGRAM ****
15 REM USE INPUTMOL TO CREATE INPUT DATA
20 REM USES FILLED CIRCLES TO REPRESENT ATOMS IN MOLECULES
```

```
30 REM HIDDEN SURFACE REPRESENTATION
40    INK 0,13:INK 1,1:MODE 1
45    INK 2,3:INK 3,9
50    PP=1000:SC=2:REM SET OBSERVER DISTANCE AND SCALE
60    INPUT"PRINT OPTION? Y OR N";P$:PT=0
70      IF P$="Y" THEN PT=1
80 DIM X(100),Y(100),Z(100),SI(100),A(4,4),SS(100),XP(100),YP(100),ZP(100)
90 LX=1000:HX=0:LY=1000:HY=0:LZ=1000:HZ=0:SZ=0:REM INITIALIZE VARIABLES
100   INPUT"INPUT DATAFILE NAME";N$
110   OPENIN N$
112   INPUT£9,H$:REM NAME OF MOLECULE
115   INPUT£9,NPTS
117 PRINT"THERE ARE" ,NPTS,"ATOMS"
120   FOR I=1 TO NPTS
130     INPUT£9,X(I),Y(I),Z(I),SI(I)
135     IF Z(I)=0 THEN Z(I)=1
140     GOSUB 4000:REM DO MIN MAX
150   NEXT I
160 CLOSEIN
170   GOSUB 4100:REM SCALE
180 REM GET AXIS FOR ROTATION
190   INPUT"INPUT AXIS FOR ROTATION: X=1,Y=2,Z=3";M
200   INPUT"INPUT ROTATION ANGLE";THETA
210   INPUT"FILL OPTION? Y OR N";P$:PS=0
220   IF P$="Y" THEN PS=1
240 FOR I=1 TO NPTS
250   XP(I)=X(I)
260   YP(I)=Y(I)
270   ZP(I)=Z(I)
280   SS(I)=SI(I)
290 NEXT I
300 REM DO ROTATION
310   THETA =THETA * 0.017455
320   GOSUB 1000:REM ROTATE SUBROUTINE
330 LX=1000:HX=0:LY=1000:HY=0:LZ=1000:HZ=0:SZ=0:REM REINITIALIZE VARIABLES
340 REM CALCULATE PROJECTION TO X,Y, PLANE
350 FOR I=1 TO NPTS
360   X4=X(I):REM X4-X8 ARE VARIABLES FOR CALCULATING PROJECTED ATOM RADII
370   X5=X4+(SI(I)/2)
380   X6=A(1,1)*X5+A(1,2)*Y(I)+A(1,3)*Z(I)+A(1,4)
390   XT=A(1,1)*X(I)+A(1,2)*Y(I)+A(1,3)*Z(I)+A(1,4)
400   YT=A(2,1)*X(I)+A(2,2)*Y(I)+A(2,3)*Z(I)+A(2,4)
410   ZT=A(3,1)*X(I)+A(3,2)*Y(I)+A(3,3)*Z(I)+A(3,4)
420   DD=ZT+PP
430   XP(I)=XT*PP/DD
440   YP(I)=YT*PP/DD
450   ZP(I)=DD
460   X4=XP(I)
470 REM NOW SET DIAMETER OF ATOM
480   X7=X6*PP/DD
490   IF X7<X4 THEN X8=X4-X7
500   IF X4<X7 THEN X8=X7-X4
510   SS(I)=(SC*X8)*2
520   IF SS(I)<0 THEN SS(I)=-SS(I)
```

```
530      GOSUB 5000:REM DO MIN MAX ON TRANSFORMED DATA
540 NEXT I
550 REM END OF PERSPECTIVE SECTION
555     CLS:REM CLEAR SCREEN
560   GOSUB 3000:REM DO SORT FOR DEPTH
562 IF M=1 THEN M$="X"
564 IF M=2 THEN M$="Y"
566 IF M=3 THEN M$="Z"
570 GA$=STR$(THETA*(1/0.017455)):LOCATE 2,25:PRINT"ANGLE="+GA$+" AXIS="M$
580   GOSUB 5100:REM DO SCALE ON TRANSFORMED DATA
590 REM NOW READY FOR PLOTTING
600   FOR I=1 TO NPTS
610      GOSUB 2000
620   NEXT I
630 K$=INKEY$:IF K$=""THEN 630
640 IF PT=1 THEN COPY
650 REM REPEAT WITH DIFFERENT VIEW
660   GOTO 180
1000 REM SUBROUTINE ROTATE
1010    C=COS(THETA)
1020    S=SIN(THETA)
1030       FOR K=1 TO 4
1040       FOR L=1 TO 4
1050         A(K,L)=0
1060       NEXT L
1070       NEXT K
1080    A(4,4)=1
1090    A(M,M)=1
1100    M1=3-M:IF M1=0 THEN M1=1
1110    M2=3:IF M=3 THEN M2=2
1120    A(M1,M1)=C
1130    A(M2,M2)=C
1140    A(M2,M1)=-S
1150    A(M1,M2)=S
1160 RETURN
2000 REM **** ROUTINE TO DRAW ATOMS ****
2010 R=SI(I):XL=XP(I):YL=YP(I):PD=1:FLAG=0
2012  LOCATE 1,1:PRINT H$
2020   IF R=50 THEN PD=2:REM SET PLOT COLOUR FOR ATOM RADIUS 15
2030   IF R=40 THEN PD=3:REM SET PLOT COLOUR FOR ATOM RADIUS 20
2035   IF R=25 THEN PD=1:REM SET PLOT COLOUR FOR ATOM RADIUS 25
2040 R=SS(I):REM NOW RESET RADIUS TO PERSPECTIVE SIZE
2050   AI=(2*PI)*(1/500)
2055   AN=-AI
2130   X1=R*COS(AN):Y1=R*SIN(AN):XS=X1:YS=Y1
2160   FOR IK=1 TO 63
2180      AN=AN+AI
2190      X1=R*COS(AN):Y1=R*SIN(AN)
2220 GOSUB 3500:REM EIGHT WAY SYMMETRY
2240   NEXT IK
2245      IF PS=0 THEN RETURN
2246 REM NOW DO FILL SECTION
2248 NN=500
2250   R=R-2
```

```
2260    X1=R*COS(AN):Y1=R*SIN(AN)
2270    XS=X1:YS=Y1
2280    X2=X1:Y2=Y1
2290    AN=AN+AI
2300    X1=R*COS(AN):Y1=R*SIN(AN)
2310    IF TEST(X1+XL,Y1+YL)>0 THEN GOTO 2350
2340    MOVE XL+X1,YL+Y1
2345    FILL PD
2350    AN=(AI*(NN/4))
2360    X1=R*COS(AN):Y1=R*SIN(AN)
2370    IF TEST(X1+XL,Y1+YL)>0 THEN GOTO 2410
2400    MOVE XL+X1,YL+Y1
2405    FILL PD
2410    AN=(AI*(NN/2))
2420    X1=R*COS(AN):Y1=R*SIN(AN)
2430    IF TEST(X1+XL,Y1+YL)>0 THEN GOTO 2470
2460    MOVE XL+X1,YL+Y1
2465    FILL PD
2470    AN=(AI*(NN*0.75))
2480    X1=R*COS(AN):Y1=R*SIN(AN)
2490    IF TEST(X1+XL,Y1+YL)>0 THEN GOTO 2540
2500    MOVE XL+X1,YL+Y1
2520    FILL PD
2540    R=R+2:RETURN
3000 REM SUBROUTINE FOR SORT
3010    FOR K=1 TO NPTS
3020    FOR J=1 TO NPTS
3030      ZZ=ZP(K)
3040      YY=YP(K)
3050      XX=XP(K)
3060      SN=SS(K):REM STORE TEMPORARY VALUES
3065      SM=SI(K)
3070      IF ZP(J)<=ZP(K) THEN 3110
3080      ZP(K)=ZP(J):ZP(J)=ZZ
3090      YP(K)=YP(J):YP(J)=YY
3100      XP(K)=XP(J):XP(J)=XX
3105      SS(K)=SS(J):SS(J)=SN
3107      SI(K)=SI(J):SI(J)=SM
3110    NEXT J
3120    NEXT K
3130 RETURN
3500 REM EIGHT WAY SYMMETRY FOR CIRCLE
3510 IF TEST(X1+XL,Y1+YL)=0 THEN PLOT X1+XL,Y1+YL ,1,0
3520 IF TEST(Y1+XL,X1+YL)=0 THEN PLOT Y1+XL,X1+YL ,1,0
3530 IF TEST(Y1+XL,-X1+YL)=0 THEN PLOT Y1+XL,-X1+YL ,1,0
3540 IF TEST(X1+XL,-Y1+YL)=0 THEN PLOT X1+XL,-Y1+YL ,1,0
3550 IF TEST(-X1+XL,-Y1+YL)=0 THEN PLOT -X1+XL,-Y1+YL ,1,0
3560 IF TEST(-Y1+XL,-X1+YL)=0 THEN PLOT-Y1+XL,-X1+YL ,1,0
3570 IF TEST(-Y1+XL,X1+YL)=0 THEN PLOT -Y1+XL,X1+YL ,1,0
3580 IF TEST(-X1+XL,Y1+YL)=0 THEN PLOT -X1+XL,Y1+YL ,1,0
3590 RETURN
4000 REM MIN MAX SUBROUTINE
4010    IF X(I)<LX THEN LX=X(I)
4020    IF X(I)>HX THEN HX=X(I)
```

```
4030    IF Y(I)<LY THEN LY=Y(I)
4040    IF Y(I)>HY THEN HY=Y(I)
4050    IF Z(I)<LZ THEN LZ=Z(I)
4060    IF Z(I)>HZ THEN HZ=Z(I)
4070    IF SI(I)>SZ THEN SZ=SI(I)
4080 RETURN
4100 REM SCALE SUBROUTINE
4105 FA=HX-LX
4110 IF (HX-LX)>(HY-LY)THEN FA=HX-LX
4120 IF (HY-LY)>(HX-LX)THEN FA=HY-LY
4130 SZ=SZ*SC:ZO=1000:ZM=0
4140    FOR I=1 TO NPTS
4150       X(I)=(X(I)-LX+1)*((640-SZ)/FA)
4155       X(I)=X(I)-320
4156       Y(I)=(Y(I)-LY+1)*((400-SZ)/FA)
4157       Y(I)=Y(I)-200
4160       Z(I)=(Z(I)-LZ+1)*((400-SZ)/FA)
4170       IF Z(I)<ZO THEN ZO=Z(I)
4180       IF Z(I)>ZM THEN ZM=Z(I)
4190    NEXT I
4200    SZ=SZ/SC
4210 RETURN
5000 REM MIN MAX SUBROUTINE FOR XP ETC
5010    IF XP(I)<LX THEN LX=XP(I)
5020    IF XP(I)>HX THEN HX=XP(I)
5030    IF YP(I)<LY THEN LY=YP(I)
5040    IF YP(I)>HY THEN HY=YP(I)
5050    IF ZP(I)<LZ THEN LZ=ZP(I)
5060    IF ZP(I)>HZ THEN HZ=ZP(I)
5070    IF SS(I)>SZ THEN SZ=SS(I)
5080 RETURN
5100 REM SCALE SUBROUTINE FOR XP ETC
5105 FA=HX-LX
5110 IF (HX-LX)>(HY-LY)THEN FA=HX-LX
5120 IF (HY-LY)>(HX-LX)THEN FA=HY-LY
5130 SZ=SZ*SC
5140    FOR I=1 TO NPTS
5150       XP(I)=(XP(I)-LX+1)*((600-SZ)/FA)
5155       XP(I)=XP(I)+(SZ/2)
5156       YP(I)=(YP(I)-LY+1)*((380-SZ)/FA)
5157       YP(I)=YP(I)+(SZ/2)
5160       ZP(I)=(ZP(I)-LZ+1)*((380-SZ)/FA)
5190    NEXT I
5200    SZ=SZ/SC
5210 RETURN
```

There is still an important component missing. A program to prepare the data is needed. A very simple program will suffice as data scaling is performed within MOL3D. The following program called INPUTMOL allows you to create a suitable file, and you can poach data from a number of sources. I have used data from the Brookhaven Data Bank: a mammoth computer collection of data from crystallographic and other sources for proteins and nucleic acids. Another good source is Wyckoff's Crystal Structures published by Wiley Interscience.

INPUTMOL program

```
10 REM **** INPUTMOL ****
20 REM CREATES DATA FOR MOL3D
30 INPUT"INPUT DATAFILE NAME";N$
40 OPENOUT N$
50 INPUT"INPUT NAME OF MOLECULE";H$
60 PRINT£9,H$
70 INPUT"NUMBER OF ATOMS";ATOMS
80 PRINT£9,ATOMS
90   FOR I=1 TO ATOMS
100     INPUT"INPUT X,Y,Z COORDS";X,Y,Z
105     INPUT"INPUT ATOM SIZE";S
110     PRINT£9,X,Y,Z,S
120   NEXT I
130 CLOSEOUT
140 END
```

And here are some pictures prepared using MOL3D.

DNA

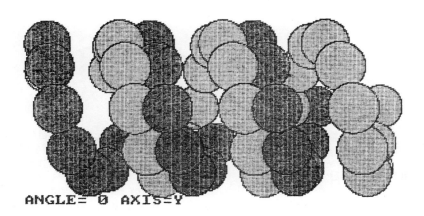

ANGLE= 0 AXIS=Y

DNA

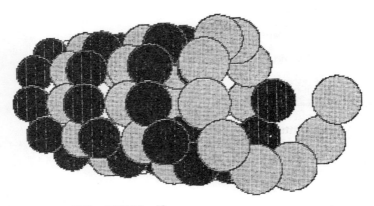

ANGLE= 50 AXIS=Y

Figure 9.4,9.5 Two views of a 'DNA double helix' with the bases on each helix shown as different coloured spheres.

OLEIC ACID

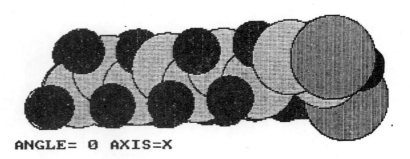

ANGLE= 0 AXIS=X

Figure 9.6 A view of the oleic acid molecule. (Data from Wyckoff, 'Crystal Structures' vol 5, Wiley Interscience). Hydrogen atoms, dark; carbon atoms stippled; oxygen atoms striped.

9.5 Some final remarks

So, congratulations! You've stayed the course to the end of this book (and I do hope that you have tried to master Appendix 2). You can be sure that much of what you've read is relevent to 'real' computer graphics, and you should be able hold your own in any conversation about pixels, refresh displays, transformations or hidden surfaces. There is no doubt that in five years time this book will be hopelessly 'underpowered'. You will then be the proud owner of a 512K memory machine with 32 bit processor, speech input, and with on-board compilers in several languages. Your future machine will have 640 X 400 pixel resolution, the ability to simultaneously display at least 256 and probably more colours from a palette of 16 million colours in high resolution mode. These specifications are undoubtably on the conservative side. Only then will you truly be able to reap the benefits of your grounding in computer graphics, but until then, make the most of your Amstrad micro!

Appendix 1
Amstrad Graphics Commands

A1.1 Overview

This appendix provides a reference guide to the graphics commands available on CPC 6128, CPC664 and CPC464 computers. Its main purpose is to save you thumbing back and forth between your User Manual and this book, but I have tried to expand on the command descriptions where it seems necessary. Some commands which affect the form of the output (for example WIDTH which changes the width of printed output) are not strictly graphics commands and they will not be discussed here. Commands specific to the CPC 6128 and CPC 664 are clearly indicated. Note that the convention for parameters specified after the commands is that those in angle brackets <> are essential, those in square brackets [ ] are optional.

A1.2 Graphic action commands

Commands in this category are the basic drawing instructions which result in graphics appearing on screen or movement of the graphics cursor. The graphics cursor can be thought of as the position of an imaginary pen head capable of movement over the screen area. The pen head can be either 'up' (ie it will move without drawing anything) or 'down' (for drawing).

```
MOVE <X coordinate>,<Y
coordinate>,[ink],[ink mode]
```

Moves the graphics cursor to the point specified by the X,Y coordinates. The ink and ink mode are optional and can be used if required. As MOVE is a 'pen up' instruction you will probably not need to specify the optional parameters (their values are discussed under DRAW below).

```
MOVER <X rel>,<Y rel>,[ink],[ink mode]
```

Moves the graphic cursor by an amount relative to the current cursor position. Relative commands are useful if you wish to use the same draw sequence at different parts of the screen.

```
DRAW <X coordinate>,<Y
coordinate>,[ink],[ink mode]
```

Draws a straight line from the current graphics cursor position to the absolute position specified in the X,Y coordinates. The Amstrad graphics firmware does this by implementation of a 'scan conversion algorithm' which works out the coordinates of all pixels along a straight line between the start and end points of the line. The optional ink parameter allows values between 0 and 15 to be specified, but note that values over one will be ignored in MODE 2 and values over three will be ignored in MODE 1.

The optional ink mode parameter was discussed in Chapter 1 and specifies how the ink being written to a pixel will interact with the existing state of the pixel.

```
DRAWR <X rel>,<Y rel>,[ink],[ink mode]
```

This is a relative draw command analogous to MOVER. It draws a line from the current graphics cursor position relative to the cursor position. It is thus possible to use negative X and/or Y coordinates if required.

```
PLOT <X coordinate>,<Y
coordinate>,[ink],[ink mode]
```

Plots a point on the screen at the X,Y coordinates specified. Note that the size of the 'point' will vary depending on the MODE chosen. With MODE 0, the point will in fact be represented on screen as four pixels parallel to the X axis. In MODE 1, the point will be two adjacent pixels parallel to the X axis, whilst only in MODE 2 will each point really be a single pixel.

```
PLOTR <X rel<,>Y rel>,[ink],[ink mode]
```

A relative version of the PLOT command.

```
CLG [ink]
```

Clears the graphics screen to the graphics paper value. If the ink colour is specified the graphics paper takes this colour. Note that CLG erases text as well as graphics! A more useful command is CLS (see 'text action' commands below) as this can be set up to erase text and not graphics.

```
FILL [ink]
```

This command works only on the CPC 6128 and CPC 664. It paints an area of the screen starting at the current screen cursor position and stops only when it reaches a boundary defined by either the current drawing ink or the paint colour. BEWARE! If the space to be filled is not totally enclosed you may find that the whole screen is painted!

A1.3 Text action commands

There is only one true text action command used in Amstrad graphics. This is the PRINT command

       PRINT [# stream], list of print items

PRINT is used for graphics printing in the same way as for normal BASIC programming. Either a literal string enclosed by quotes, for example

       PRINT "GRAPH LABEL"

or a variable, for example

       PRINT A$

can be used. Items separated by commas or semicolons can also be put in the same statement.

       TAG [# stream]

'frees' printed output from the text screen positions and instead specifies that text printing will begin at the current graphics cursor location. TAG is in fact an acronym for Text At Graphics. All PRINTed items should end with a semicolon to suppress printing of control characters (eg line feed and carriage return). To return to normal text mode the command

       TAGOFF [# stream]

is used. Text then begins at the last text cursor position.

A1.4 Graphics environmental commands

Environmental commands affect the 'environment' of graphic action commands. They include commands specifying colour, MODE and relocation of the origin.

We will first consider the colour commands. Note that the default inks for background and drawing colours are 0 and 1 respectively. This means that you can change the screen or pen colour merely by specifying an ink number of 0 or 1 with the appropriate colour code. For graphic applications that do not need more than two colours, you only need to use the INK command

    BORDER <colour>, [flash colour]

This command sets the screen border colour. The colour chosen is completely independent of the colours used in the mainscreen area, so even in MODE 2, any of the available 27 colours can be specified for the border. The optional flash colour will flash with the primary border colour (ugh!) at a rate set by the SPEED INK command.

    INK <number>, <colour>, [colour]

One of the difficulties in getting to grips with Amstrad graphics is the relationship between ink colours and ink numbers. Although there are 27 possible colours available, they cannot be referred to directly by colour number but must first be assigned code numbers. These numbers are then used to refer to the colours in the PAPER and PEN commands (see below). You cannot therefore specify

    PAPER 22

expecting to get a pastel green text background! Instead you must use

    INK 2,22
    GRAPHICS PAPER 2

There are two remaining colour commands that are specific to non-text graphics. These are GRAPHICS PAPER and GRAPHICS PEN.

    GRAPHICS PAPER <INk>

This sets the colour of the area behind graphics drawn on screen. This command is only useful in a few instances, for example if a dashed line is to be drawn using the MASK command

    GRAPHICS PEN [ink], [background mode]

GRAPHICS PEN sets the graphics pen colour in exactly the same way as the PEN command sets the text pen colour.

    MODE <type>

MODE affects the appearance of text. The characteristics of the three permissible modes are as follows.

Mode	Pixel Size	Character Size	Inks
0	160 X 200	20 X 25	16
1	320 X 200	40 X 25	4
2	640 X 200	80 X 25	2

The 'true' number of pixels on your monitor is actually 640 X 200 and MODEs 0 and 1 overcome this apparent discrepancy by addressing more than one pixel in the horizontal direction for each coordinate point specified. Try plotting

PLOT 0,0

for example in **MODE 1**. If your eyesight is good you will see that two adjacent pixels (0,0 and 1,0) are actually lit on screen. Now switch to **MODE 0** and **PLOT** the same point. Four pixels are now lit (0,0; 1,0; 2,0 and 3,0). If you try to plot any of these four pixels you will find that, in **MODE 0**, the same bar of four pixels is always lit. Only when you **PLOT 4,0** will the next bar of four pixels appear! This apparent overlap is the cause of the low definition available in **MODE 0**.

MASK [integer in range 0-55], [start mode]

MASK is specific to the CPC 6128 and CPC 664 and sets the dash pattern for a line. This command is considered at greater length in Chapter 2

ORIGIN <X coordinate>, <Y coordinate>, [left, right, top, bottom]

This command is used if you wish to move the screen origin (ie pixel 0,0) away from the left hand lower corner of the screen. If an **ORIGIN** of 100,100 is set, the effective screen coordinate system is X -100,540 and Y -100,300. The optional parameters can be used to set up a 'clipping area' outside which non-text graphics and TAGged text will not be written.

The CPC 6128 has two additional commands to copy the screen contents back and forth between the visible screen and the second 64K bank of memory present on this machine. We have seen in earlier chapters that the screen occupies 16K of memory, and in fact four separate screenfuls of information can be stored in the 'spare' 64K of memory on the CPC 6128. The relevant commands are called **SCREENSWAP** (to exchange contents of different 16K memory blocks), and **SCREENCOPY** to copy the information making up one screen into any one of the alternate 16K memory blocks). These commands will probably prove of great use to games programmers, but the wider value is questionnable.

A1.5 Text environmental commands

These affect the appearance of text on screen. The relevent Amstrad commands are those for colour changes and text location.

        PAPER [# stream], <ink>

Sets the colour for text cells. As with all other commands with the optional stream parameter, a default of stream #0 is assumed. Unlike BORDER, the number of inks available are limited by the MODE in use.

        PEN [# stream], [ink], [background mode]

This command only changes the colour of the text on screen, non-text graphics remaining unaffected. Both 'ink' and 'background mode' are optional, but one must be specified. 'Background mode' sets the relationship between text and other graphics on the screen. If the MODE is set to 0, the text cells will overwrite any graphics encountered by text. If MODE 1 is specified only text characters and not text cells will overwrite graphics.

        LOCATE [#stream], <column>, <row>

LOCATE allows you to set the position of the text cursor to the point specified by the column and row coordinates.

        WINDOW [#stream], <left col, right col, top
        row, bottom row>

Text windows can be created using the WINDOW command. If the stream is not specified, the normal output stream of 0 is used by default. Note that the window size should be consistent with the MODE in use (eg don't use a right column value of < 40 when in MODE 1)

Appendix 2
Matrix Manipulation

A2.1 What are matrices?

This appendix details the matrix operations necessary to carry out both two and three dimensional rotation translation and scaling. You can use the information here to help you to understand the routines in the earlier chapters of the book, or alternatively as the base for your own programs. It is not strictly necessary to use matrices to carry out transformations on coordinate data. As you will have seen from some of the examples discussed earlier, algebraic equations can be derived to carry out the manipulations needed, and matrices are simply an alternative way of doing the calculations. The use of matrices makes things a lot simpler when it comes to handling three dimensions, and it is therefore a useful skill to acquire even when handling two dimensions. Matrix algebra is suited to computer solution. Whereas humans like to deal with information in a linear fashion (a then b then c and so on), computers can easily handle information in tabular (=array) format, and this is really what matrices are all about. In essence, matrices are tabular representations of algebraic equations.

2.2 Two dimensional transformations

Let us represent a point in two dimensional space as a column vector

$$\begin{bmatrix} x \\ y \\ 1 \end{bmatrix}$$

The meaning of x and y are clear - they are the x and y coordinates of the point. The '1' is in the vector because in mathematical terms we are dealing with 'homogeneous coordinates' - but forget this for the present. We can write the matrices for transformations in two dimensional space in the following way:

For *rotation*

$$\begin{bmatrix} \cos A & \sin A & 0 \\ -\sin A & \cos A & 0 \\ 0 & 0 & 1 \end{bmatrix}$$

where A is the (clockwise) angle of rotation about the origin

For *scaling*

$$\begin{bmatrix} SX & 0 & 0 \\ 0 & SY & 0 \\ 0 & 0 & 1 \end{bmatrix}$$

where SX,SY are the scale factors for the X and Y axes respectively

For *translation*

$$\begin{bmatrix} 1 & 0 & TX \\ 0 & 1 & TY \\ 0 & 0 & 0 \end{bmatrix}$$

where TX,TY are the X and Y translations

If you wish to apply one of these transformations alone, then matrix multiplication of the coordinate vector and the corresponding transformation matrix must be performed.

The BASIC code to do this multiplication is easier than the theory behind it! Assuming that the transformation matrix is in the 3 X 3 array A(3,3), and the coordinate points are X=PO(1),Y=PO(2),1=PO(3)

```
10   REM **** MATRIX MULTIPLICATION 1 ****
20   FOR I=1 TO 3
30   FOR J=1 TO 3
40   P(I)=A(I,J)*PO(J)
50   NEXT J
60   NEXT I
```

The result is stored in the array P, so the new X and Y values are in P(1) and P(2) respectively. You will have seen code of this general structure used in, for example TRANSFORMV2 (Chapter 4), in lines 510-575. In this program, the transformed X and Y coordinates are obtained from the array P (lines 565-570).

One of the major advantages of using matrices is the possibility of premultiplying separate transformation matrices so that only one multiplication of the coordinate data like the one above has to be done. Instead of the (3 X 1) and (3 X 3) matrices being multiplied, in this case we multiply two (3 X 3) matrices. For example we may wish to translate an object to the origin, to rotate it by a given angle, and then to translate it back to the original position. Instead of two intermediate calculations of the transformed coordinate data, the three matrices needed to carry out the whole transformation can be multiplied amongst themselves.

Multiplying two 3 X 3 matrices together is carried out easily enough in BASIC. If A and B are the matrices to be multiplied, the result of multiplying them together is another 3 X 3 matrix, C. The multiplication is as follows

```
10    REM **** MATRIX MULTIPLICATION 2 ****
20    FOR I=1 TO 3
30    FOR J=1 TO 3
40    FOR K=1 TO 3
50    C(I,J)=A(I,K)*B(K,J)
60    NEXTK
70    NEXTJ
80    NEXTI
```

What this short routine actually does, is to multiply row I of the first matrix by column J of the second matrix. You can see this code in action in TRV3 C hapter 4 again), lines 1600-1790.

Let us now put all this together to do a typical series of transformations. The diagram below shows an example set of transformations on a triangle. These are:

(1)   Increase the Y scale by a factor of two.

(2)   Rotate the axes through 45 degrees (= pi/4 radians).

(3)   Move the origin by 50 X, 100 Y.

We therefore need the following 3 X 3 matrices

$$S = \begin{bmatrix} 1 & 0 & 0 \\ 0 & 2 & 0 \\ 0 & 0 & 1 \end{bmatrix}$$

$$R = \begin{bmatrix} .7071 & .7071 & 0 \\ -.7071 & .7071 & 0 \\ 0 & 0 & 1 \end{bmatrix}$$

$$T = \begin{bmatrix} 1 & 0 & 50 \\ 0 & 1 & 100 \\ 0 & 0 & 0 \end{bmatrix}$$

The complete transformation is obtained by multiplying the matrices, so we need the result of

$$\begin{bmatrix} 1 & 0 & 0 \\ 0 & 2 & 1 \\ 0 & 0 & 1 \end{bmatrix} \times \begin{bmatrix} .7071 & .7071 & 0 \\ -.7071 & .7071 & 0 \\ 0 & 0 & 1 \end{bmatrix} \times \begin{bmatrix} 1 & 0 & 50 \\ 0 & 1 & 100 \\ 0 & 0 & 0 \end{bmatrix}$$

We have already looked at the BASIC code that will carry out matrix multiplication for us. It will be clear to you from this code that only two matrices can be multiplied at once, and this would be expected from the normal laws of multiplication. But here the similarity with normal multiplication ends, because in matrix terms, 6 X 3 does not equal 3 X 6! Matrix multiplication is achieved by the following method. First, work across each column of the first matrix from left to right like this

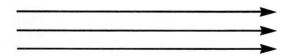

Multiply each element of the matrix by the next downwards element in the second matrix. You therefore work through the second matrix like this

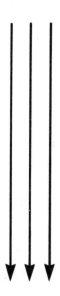

So for matrices A and B with the elements written like this

$$\begin{bmatrix} A_{11} & A_{12} & A_{13} \\ A_{21} & A_{22} & A_{23} \\ A_{31} & A_{32} & A_{33} \end{bmatrix} \begin{bmatrix} B_{11} & B_{12} & B_{13} \\ B_{21} & B_{22} & B_{23} \\ B_{31} & B_{32} & B_{33} \end{bmatrix}$$

To calculate the first column of the product matrix C, the following is done

$$(A_{11} B_{11}) + (A_{12} B_{21}) + (A_{13} B_{31})$$

which is the same as

(row1 X column1)

$$(A_{21} B_{11}) + (A_{22} B_{21}) + (A_{23} B_{31})$$

which is the same as

(row2 X column1)

$$(A_{31} B_{11}) + (A_{32} B_{21}) + (A_{33} B_{31})$$

which is the same as

(row3 X column1)

so the 'master plan' for the matrix multiplication is:

row1 X column1	row1 X column2	row1 X column3
row2 X column1	row2 X column2	row2 X column3
row3 X column1	row3 X column2	row3 X column3

You might like to try multiplying the numbers from our transformation example to check that you have understood all this. First multiply the rotation and translation matrices. Then multiply the product by the scaling matrix

You should get the following result

$$\begin{bmatrix} .7071 & .7071 & 106.055 \\ -1.414 & 1.414 & 70.71 \\ 0 & 0 & 0 \end{bmatrix}$$

There is one thing to watch while doing these multiplications, and that is the order in which the multiplications are done. If you do them in the wrong order, or try to multiply B by A instead of A by B, you will get into trouble. As a general rule, always multiply in the following order.

ROTATION X TRANSLATION → PRODUCT1

SCALE X PRODUCT1 → PRODUCT2

In order to transform the coordinates of our example triangle, the column vector for each pair of x y coordinates is multiplied by the matrix PRODUCT2, as we saw earlier in this appendix. So to transform the point X=70, Y=25, you would calculate the result of

$$
\begin{bmatrix}
.7071 & .7071 & 106.055 \\
-1.414 & 1.414 & 70.71 \\
0 & 0 & 1
\end{bmatrix}
\quad X \quad
\begin{bmatrix}
70 \\
25 \\
1
\end{bmatrix}
$$

For completeness, you might like to work through the arithmetic to do this (the faint hearted can take refuge in the fact that we have already seen the BASIC code to do the job!) With the nomenclature we used for the (3 X 3) X (3 X 3) case, we have

$$
\begin{bmatrix}
A_{11} & A_{12} & A_{13} \\
A_{21} & A_{22} & A_{23} \\
A_{31} & A_{32} & A_{33}
\end{bmatrix}
\quad X \quad
\begin{bmatrix}
B_{11} \\
B_{21} \\
B_{31}
\end{bmatrix}
$$

and this becomes

$$
\begin{bmatrix}
A_{11}B_{11} + A_{12}B_{21} + A_{13}B_{31} \\
A_{21}B_{11} + A_{22}B_{21} + A_{23}B_{31} \\
A_{31}B_{11} + A_{32}B_{21} + A_{33}B_{31}
\end{bmatrix}
$$

so the column vector product becomes

$$\begin{bmatrix} 212.1 \\ 141.4 \\ 1 \end{bmatrix}$$

and the point 70,25 is therefore transformed to 212.1, 141.4.

Now look at the effect of applying the transformation matrices for the whole triangle

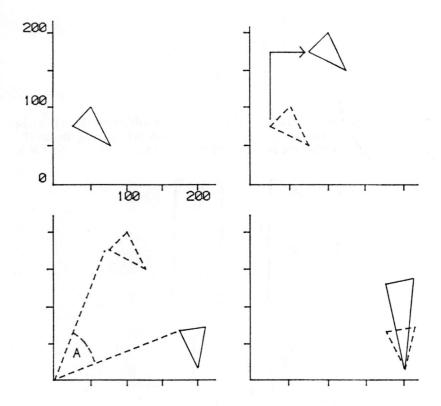

Figure A2.1 Transformations on a triangle. Top left, untransformed triangle. Top right, translation by +50,+100; bottom left, rotation around origin by 45 degrees; bottom right, scaling by a factor of two on the Y axis.

A2.3 Three dimensional transformations

The difficulties of visualising transformations in three dimensions have already been alluded to in Chapter 7. We have seen how the three main types of transformation can be represented in matrix format in two dimensions, and with relatively little extra effort matrices can also be used to represent 3D transformations. In three dimensions, our single point coordinates are written in the form of a column vector

$$\begin{bmatrix} X \\ Y \\ Z \\ 1 \end{bmatrix}$$

and each transformation matrix is 4 X 4 instead of 3 X 3 in size.

The rules for multiplication are exactly the same as with two dimensions, so all that is left really is to list the relevent matrices. These are

For *scaling*

$$S = \begin{bmatrix} SX & 0 & 0 & 0 \\ 0 & SY & 0 & 0 \\ 0 & 0 & SZ & 0 \\ 0 & 0 & 0 & 1 \end{bmatrix}$$

For *translation*

$$T = \begin{bmatrix} 1 & 0 & 0 & TX \\ 0 & 1 & 0 & TY \\ 0 & 0 & 1 & TZ \\ 0 & 0 & 0 & 1 \end{bmatrix}$$

For rotation, things are a little more complicated. Because we are adrift in three dimensional space, we need to be a little more specific about just what we mean by rotation (we looked at this problem in Chapter 7). To obtain rotation about a single axis, we can use one of the following matrices

For X

$$
\begin{bmatrix}
1 & 0 & 0 & 0 \\
0 & \cos A & \sin A & 0 \\
0 & -\sin A & \cos A & 0 \\
0 & 0 & 0 & 1
\end{bmatrix}
$$

For Y

$$
\begin{bmatrix}
\cos A & 0 & -\sin A & 0 \\
0 & 1 & 0 & 0 \\
\sin A & 0 & \cos A & 0 \\
0 & 0 & 0 & 1
\end{bmatrix}
$$

For Z

$$
\begin{bmatrix}
\cos A & \sin A & 0 & 0 \\
-\sin A & \cos A & 0 & 0 \\
0 & 0 & 1 & 0 \\
0 & 0 & 0 & 1
\end{bmatrix}
$$

Subroutine ROTATE in program TRANS3D (Chapter 7) was based on these matrices. You will note that a little juggling with the values in the variable M in ROTATE enables any of the three matrices to be set up by specifying a single integer in the range 1 - 3.

Appendix 3

References on Computer Graphics.

There are many books available on computer graphics, and now that you have explored some simple graphics techniques on your Amstrad you might like to investigate the literature. I have made use of all the books listed in this Appendix, and I recommend them for your attention. The level of treatment of graphics topics varies extensively from book to book, so note my remarks carefully lest you spend hard earned cash on a book that doesn't address your own interests!

Angell, I O *(1981) A Practical Introduction to Computer Graphics. Macmillan*

This is a very clear introduction to graphics which deals with many of the concepts introduced here, covering them in more detail. The programming examples are given in Fortran, assuming that the reader has access to a graphics package on a 'traditional' mini or mainframe computer. Nevertheless, this book is very useful if you want a gentle method of learning more about computer graphics techniques.

Giloh, W G *(1978) Interactive Computer Graphics. Prentice Hall*

Real hair-shirt stuff this. Giloh's book is something of a classic in the more mathematical and algorithmic aspects of graphics programming. Half the book concerns itself with graphics data structures. If you want to get into heavy theory, this book will show you the way.

Foley J D and Van Dam A *(1982) Fundamentals of Interactive Computer Graphics. Addison Wesley*

This is one of those textbooks that only the Americans know how to produce. Beautifully laid out, it covers everything you need for a complete overview of graphics hard and software, using Pascal for the programming examples. It will tell you everything from the detailed analysis of user-interactive design packages to the ins and outs of the 'state of the art' Evans and Sutherland PictureSystem 200.

Rogers D G and Adams J A *(1976) Mathematical Elements for Computer Graphics. McGraw-Hill*

This book covers the mathematics of graphics in great detail, yet in a way that is microcomputer oriented (all the example subroutines are in BASIC). Quite helpful, but only if you are into the mathematical side of graphics.

Hearn D and Baker M P *(1984) Microcomputer Graphics: Techniques and Applications. Prentice Hall Inc*

An excellent book for the novice or graphics buff working on a home computer. This book is a little on the simple side, and many of the techniques discussed in the present book will also be found in Hearn and Baker. These authors have done an excellent job in producing a book that can be read by users of any microcomputer with graphics capability.

Mufti A A *(1983) Elementary Computer Graphics. Prentice Hall Inc*

Quite an elementary text, but not much fun to read. Perhaps this book would be useful for science and engineering based students rather than a home audience.

Newman W M and Sproull R F *(1981) Principles of Interactive Computer Graphics. McGraw Hill Inc*

This book was the most complete introduction to computer graphics until Foley and Van Dam entered the scene. Although it is a less pretty book and is less up-to-date than Foley and Van Dam many sections are explained more clearly and simply, especially the parts on hidden lines and surfaces.

Artwick B A *(1984) Applied Concepts in Microcomputer Graphics. Prentice Hall Inc*

This is a very individual book, and covers a lot of material skimmed over in other books: it has a lot of detail on microcomputer graphics hardware, for example. A good book for the dedicated graphics programmer to mull over.

INDEX